HUMAN
BEINGS
FIRST

PRACTICES *for*
EMPATHETIC, EXPRESSIVE
LEADERSHIP

PAUL E. WOLFE

For permission requests, write to the publisher, addressed "Attention: Permissions Coordinator," at the address below.

Publish Your Purpose
141 Weston Street, #155
Hartford, CT, 06141

The opinions expressed by the Author are not necessarily those held by Publish Your Purpose.

Ordering Information: Quantity sales and special discounts are available on quantity purchases by corporations, associations, and others. For details, contact the publisher at hello@publishyourpurpose.com.

Edited by: Candi S. Cross, Blue DuLac, Caroline Davis
Cover design by: INDIVIDUAL™
Author Photo: ©Saami Bloom, 2022
Typeset by: Medlar Publishing Solutions Pvt Ltd., India

Printed in the United States of America.

ISBN: 979-8-88797-017-2 (hardcover)
ISBN: 979-8-88797-016-5 (paperback)
ISBN: 979-8-88797-018-9 (ebook)

Library of Congress Control Number: 2022921972

First edition, February 2023.

The information contained within this book is strictly for informational purposes. The material may include information, products, or services by third parties. As such, the Author and Publisher do not assume responsibility or liability for any third-party material or opinions. The publisher is not responsible for websites (or their content) that are not owned by the publisher. Readers are advised to do their own due diligence when it comes to making decisions.

Publish Your Purpose is a hybrid publisher of non-fiction books. Our mission is to elevate the voices often excluded from traditional publishing. We intentionally seek out authors and storytellers with diverse backgrounds, life experiences, and unique perspectives to publish books that will make an impact in the world. Do you have a book idea you would like us to consider publishing? Please visit PublishYourPurpose.com for more information.

Contents

Acknowledgments .... *ix*

Introduction – The Great Return .... *xi*

Chapter 1 – Reflect 1

Chapter 2 – Share 15

Chapter 3 – See 29

Chapter 4 – Listen 43

Chapter 5 – Care 59

Chapter 6 – Connect 69

Chapter 7 – Help... 87

Chapter 8 – Protect.. 101

Conclusion – Being Better ‖ Better Being 113

Bibliography 117

About the Author 123

Work With Paul 125

Acknowledgments

Writing a book can be difficult. As a first-time author, I was unsure of how to get started or what it would take to complete. But having great friends, family, and mentors certainly helps. This book is about leadership, more specifically better leadership. Truly, at its core, it is about all of us as Human Beings. We cannot become better until we all fully embrace who we are.

I would most like to thank my mom. She was killed thirty years ago, but I learned so much from her as I was growing up and into my early adulthood. My mom was driven and passionate about educating children, selfless and bold as a single parent, and all the things you would want in a mom; especially growing up gay in North Miami, Florida. I hope she is proud of me.

Drew, my husband, my friend, my partner in life, thank you for being you. You embrace me as I am—all the good, bad, and ugly. You are supportive—even though at times I know you think my ideas are out there. I am so lucky to have been on this ride with you for almost thirty years, and I hope there are many more decades of fun to come.

Thank you, Pam, for being an amazing best friend. Who knew that we would still be here almost thirty years later after being introduced at the mailbox in Jacaranda Pointe? I appreciate your support, transparency, and friendship.

Nolan Farris—or should I call you "Moldy?"—thanks for embracing the fact that I dropped the "F" bomb with you in my interview for my role at Indeed. I appreciate your friendship, humor, and guidance.

Thanks to Erin Weed, for being an amazing human who helped me understand myself "better." Your work helped me determine the premise of this book.

To my co-writer, Candi Cross, thank you for making my stories and teachings have a real impact, helping me develop the content for this book, and making it fun along the way. Thank you to our experts: Irene Brank, Nolan Farris, Maureen Lippe, Greg Morley, Irina Soriano, and Ekta Vyas for their wisdom and vulnerability, expressive and empathetic leadership, as well as for setting and sharing the examples I have shared in this book for readers.

To Jenn Grace and the team at Publish Your Purpose, I appreciate all of you and all that you do to help authors bring their stories to life.

Finally, thanks to everyone I have had the pleasure of working with over the last thirty years. Many of you have made me a better leader, employee, and Human Being.

*"If your actions inspire others
to dream more, learn more, do more
and become more, you are a leader."*

—JOHN QUINCY ADAMS,
6th President of the United States

The Great Return

I am not a scientist, but I agree with the findings of the Wisconsin School of Business about the chemicals of leadership and their biological impact.[1] When you are kind to someone, your heart swells. When you hear gratifying words, your immune system gets a boost and it is better able to deal with the stressors of the day. Based on what I have seen and heard over my twenty years as an HR executive at multinational companies, I wish we all could experience a daily dose of this positivity! However, we have been busy with the shuffle of getting ahead, climbing the ladder, and making impossible demands on ourselves and others in order to prove our worth and that we are not

---

[1] Barry Roberts, "Understanding the Chemicals of Leadership and the Impact They Can Have," Wisconsin School of Business, June 15, 2016, https://business.wisc.edu/news/understanding-the-chemicals-of-leadership-and-the-impact-they-can-have/.

imposters. Yet, we have discovered that our bodies house four important chemicals that add to our success in business and in life. According to Barry Roberts, custom program manager for the Center for Professional and Executive Development at the Wisconsin School of Business, they are:

Endorphins: Mask physical pain and promote feelings of happiness. Physical exercise is a good endorphin-producing activity, but the positive feelings are very short-lived. A company party, picnic, or other celebration helps raise morale but only temporarily.

Dopamine: Contributes to the feeling of accomplishment and elation from completing a task, achieving a goal, or winning in a game. This is why checking a completed task off a list feels good. Because we seek the positive feelings of dopamine, it can enable us to stay focused, but if left unbalanced, it can be dangerous and lead to addictive behaviors such as gambling or excessive video gaming. Having clear goals for employees and progress or achievement scorecards helps leaders stimulate dopamine in a constructive way.

Oxytocin: Invokes feelings of love and loyalty. This chemical drives us to be around people we like and trust. Oxytocin is produced through human touch and acts of kindness or generosity. For leaders, being authentic and transparent are trustworthy behaviors that can also produce oxytocin and promote admiration and loyalty in others.

Serotonin: Supports a sense of pride, status, and gratitude. From a leadership lens, this means that when employees feel that their leader has their back, in turn, they will take care of their leader, the company, and each other.

How do we get all of these flowing all the time? Roberts talks about a fifth chemical, **cortisol**, also known as the stress hormone. Our bodies have surely been manufacturing cortisol in record amounts over the past three years—the pandemic era. He writes,

> *Individuals choose different strategies to manage stress, from destructive behaviors such as smoking and drinking alcohol to constructive strategies such as mindfulness meditation and physical exercise. Leaders need to recognize how their behavior, expectations, and decisions can increase stress to unhealthy levels for others, and then make changes to foster a truly healthy environment and culture. We can also teach the skills needed for individuals to reduce stress and cortisol constructively regardless of their role in the organization.*

We have a choice to make as leaders. Do we take care of our needs in positive ways, allowing us to reach peak performance and, hopefully, get our team there too? Or instead, do we allow these chemicals in our bodies, that produce such strong feelings and the reactions that come with them, to get out of control?

The choice is ours. I want to experience my endorphins, dopamine, oxytocin, serotonin, and cortisol in the most positive way possible. Doing this is what will allow me to become a better leader for my team and a better human being.

As human beings, we contain a world of power in just our emotions alone. We are emotional creatures, regardless of whether we display those emotions as leaders. Let's break down that power.

From Resignation to Return

In 2021, forty million people took part in the Great Resignation, putting up permanent Out of Office notes at their workplaces and running for the exit signs.[2] It was not due to working conditions alone, nor was it a search for certainty or self-fulfillment due to the COVID-19 pandemic, as was generously reported. According to a study published in the *MIT Sloan Management Review*,[3] researchers discovered the record turnover was driven by a pervasive desire to leave toxic work cultures. From data collected between April and September 2021, consisting of Glassdoor reviews (including some written before the pandemic) and 172 culture metrics for roughly six hundred companies, researchers found toxic work culture to be the most reported factor in the decision to quit. The same study also found that a toxic work culture was 10 times more important than pay in predicting turnover. Abusive leaders and cutthroat environments, where employees felt colleagues were actively undermining them, capped the top five of the list grievances that created and intensified a toxic work culture.

Let that sink in—workplace culture was valued as 10 times more important than compensation. Also noteworthy: the data collected is about the overall corporate culture; imagine if they looked at team or department culture, or even just the direct relationship between employee and leader. There is a saying that floats around in corporate America: "People don't leave

---

[2] Emma Goldberg, "All of Those Quitters? They're at Work." *The New York Times*, May 13, 2022, https://www.nytimes.com/2022/05/13/business/great-resignation-jobs.html.
[3] Donald Sull, Charles Sull, and Ben Zweig, "Toxic Culture Is Driving the Great Resignation." *MIT Sloan Management Review*, January 11, 2022, https://sloanreview.mit.edu/article/toxic-culture-is-driving-the-great-resignation/.

companies, they leave bosses." I believe it! Based on this research, it seems that they probably leave for both reasons.

The seismic impact of a bad leader does not need to be spelled out for you. Our bodies have been impacted by bad leaders in the most debilitating ways. Stress and anxiety from work can trigger PTSD and cause (or worsen) at least nine possible illnesses.[4]

This is alarming, but there is a way forward. We can make amends by being empathetic and expressive leaders amid the Great Return, during which millions have rejoined the workforce. In March 2022, the U.S. economy added 431,000 jobs, taking the unemployment rate to a new pandemic-era low of 3.6 percent. That is just a tad above the unemployment rate before the pandemic.[5]

My word for this electrifying period of reassessment is *better*. Let's be better. Let's empathize better. Let's express ourselves better. Being *better* is far less pressure laden (and at times, maniacal) than being *the best*. If we all strived to do better in every interaction with our employees, we could celebrate and cement this Great Return. Not to mention that we would be strong enough to weather any forthcoming crises together; the more formidable challenges of our era that require emotional and mental antibodies to stave off another Great Resignation.

The business world has lost sight of the golden rule we learned in kindergarten: Treat others as *you* want to be treated. We could evolve this definition as adults and leaders. Consider this book

[4] Jenny Splitter, "9 Ways Stress Can Make You Sick," *Everyday Health*, May 19, 2022, https://www.everydayhealth.com/emotional-health/stress/illnesses-caused-stress/.
[5] Meghan Biro, "Great Employee Return—Or Big Employer Mistake?" *Forbes*, April 4, 2022, https://www.forbes.com/sites/meghanbiro/2022/04/04/great-employee-return---or-big-employer-mistake/.

an extended version of it. My biggest objective is to become a better leader, a better human being. I do not believe that it is difficult, especially if we graduate from the golden rule to the platinum rule. Treat others as *they* want to be treated. I care about people and I want everyone to feel seen. If everyone made a concerted effort to treat one person better, wouldn't that be amazing? It would be exponentially better for everyone, a utopia at some point. *Seeing is believing*–the belief we have in who we are seeing and the glow someone emits when you really see them. I like Caleb Madison's definition of feeling seen. He asserts in *The Atlantic*:

> *I don't think we mean* seen *as in 'viewed.' I can't imagine someone receiving a relatable meme from a friend and responding, 'I feel famous.' It's also not* seen *as in 'watched.' We're not smashing that 'Like' button and laughing because the government is watching us through our front-facing iPhone cameras. It's more like 'I feel understood' or 'I feel affirmed' or 'I feel recognized.' It's a feeling of identification with the content that has truthfully reflected our own experience back to us, like Narcissus, staring at his own image in the lake, feeling so seen right now.*[6]

Empathetic, expressive leadership is not a new mission for me. It started in the late '80s and early '90s, as I worked in customer service at call centers for companies such as American Express and GE. In the late '90s, I managed a customer service department for CitySearch, an online guide that provides information about businesses. It exists to this day, and focuses

---

[6] Caleb Madison, "That Feeling When You 'Feel Seen'," *The Atlantic*, December 20, 2021, https://www.theatlantic.com/newsletters/archive/2021/12/that-feeling-when-you-feel-seen/621050/.

on the categories of dining, entertainment, retail, travel, and professional services in cities throughout the United States. It had an exciting, young spirit in the Internet's heyday, and people were hungry and ambitious.

Two years in, the company asked me to run their HR department. I said, "You're out of your f**king minds." Their sell to me was, "You're smart, a respected leader, and you understand our business." Over two or three weeks of conversations and meals in May of 2000, I agreed to lead the HR department for six months. My only caveat was, "If I'm terrible, you have to give me another job in the company." That was twenty-two years ago. I still thank them because I would not want to be running call centers now.

Overall, customer service and HR are not that different when it comes to people-focused tasks. Consider a customer service leader who pioneers measurable standards for the department. These new standards influence customer satisfaction, such as responding to an inquiry within a set timescale, resolving a customer problem, or reducing the number of times a customer calls with the same issue. This creates a process for monitoring and measuring service staff, and it devises procedures for escalating a problem to a more senior staff member if necessary. In this case, that senior staff member was usually me.

With this lens, customer service requires active listening, empathy, and sympathy at times. I needed to be a mediator between what the company and customers wanted by finding a resolution that everyone was somewhat happy with. In HR, while you have a legal component (labor laws, Fair Labor Standards Act, and the Family and Medical Leave Act), you often play the role of mediator or therapist. Sometimes people simply want to be heard.

That alone could be what people need to move forward—to be heard and understood. They want to know that you understand how something made them feel, that you can relate to them in some way, and that you can empathize with them. Working in HR means that my employees are my "customers." When my thousands of customers and I experienced a once-in-a-lifetime pandemic simultaneously, I was called to shine a bright light on empathetic, expressive leadership at a time when it was needed the most.

Summoning the Strength to Be Better

In mid-February 2020, I was in Austin, Texas, for a week of meetings, and we had been hearing rumblings of COVID-19 in the Asia-Pacific region. We had offices all over the globe and when I landed in New York, I received a text from one of our HR business partners in Singapore. The wife and son of one of our employees had been at a doctor's office where a case had been confirmed. They had potentially been exposed, and in the very early days of COVID-19 we did not have much information. It was midnight my time when I texted my boss, our Chief Operating Officer. I did not hear back, so I texted our Chief Executive Officer.

When our CEO responded I called and informed him of everything I knew. Sadly, that was next to nothing, but my alarm bells were sounding. I was responsible for the health and safety of eleven thousand people. Our plan was that I would send a note to our employees in Singapore explaining the situation, and we would close that office until we knew more. We didn't know if or where it would hit next, and we had employees traveling all the time to many different locations.

On March 2, we held a senior leadership team meeting to discuss COVID-19. Our COO said we should close all of our offices, and have the employees work from home until we had a better handle on things. We were a data-driven company, clamoring for data that didn't exist. Still, we were in a time of rapid emotional upheaval.

Like so many others, COVID-19 affected my personal life as well. My in-laws in Columbus, Ohio, both caught COVID-19 before the vaccines were developed. The complications severely affected my mother-in-law's physical and cognitive abilities. She was in and out of hospitals and nursing homes for over four months. No visitors were allowed until her final ten days. Even then, only my husband, his father, his aunt, and his siblings were permitted to visit due to COVID-19 protocols and restrictions.

I heard what my employees were going through and I could relate. I shared their questions and fears. We all have personal lives. We are all human beings first. The line between life and work did not exist anymore.

All leaders can, and should, utilize their empathy and life experiences to build (and continuously improve) their work relationships. We have had the same paradigm of work and leadership for so long, but now we know you do not have to show up at an office to be a strong leader. You do not have to keep everything bottled up inside. You do not have to hold all the answers.

After almost two years of developing and adapting to the new norms of the global work environment while guiding the organization through how these changes affected employment, leadership, coaching, and benefits, I found myself re-evaluating my career priorities. Although I was ready to be part of the Great Resignation, I was really ready to be part of something more. I prefer to think of it as the Great Reassessment—one in which we analyze every area of our lives (not just the professional area) as if it were a pie chart laid out before us. We can examine the time we've been spending on each area and reassess how much time we'd prefer to spend on work moving forward. Now we have new priorities, and we are trying to figure out how we can reconfigure our Time Pie for a Great Return—to something.

Writing for *Fortune*, Ranjay Gulati calls it a "Great Rethink," in which we are all rethinking our relationship to work and how it fits into our lives.

> There is abundant research to show that employees of all ages want jobs that are not merely interesting and reasonably compensated, but meaningful and purposeful. A recent McKinsey survey of employees found that 89 percent desired a sense of purpose at work. Recognizing how much both customers and employees value a sense of purpose, many companies have developed and promoted inspiring purpose or mission statements.
>
> It's no longer enough to build and sell cars. You must instead purport, as Ford Motor Company does, to 'build a better world, where every person is free to move and pursue their dreams.' It's no longer enough to sell coffee. Like Starbucks, you must 'inspire and nurture the human spirit—one person, one cup, and one neighborhood at a time.'[7]

---

[7] Ranjay Gulati, "It's not a Great Resignation–it's a Great Rethink," *Fortune*, March 8, 2022, https://fortune.com/2022/03/08/great-resignation-careers-rethink-labor-shortage-pandemic-work-ranjay-gulati/.

We are all human beings who think and rethink, that's for sure! Thinking about my personal rebrand as I dove into my Great Reassessment, it was similar to the big brands. I may have consumed a lot of coffee, too.

When I told my peers and team, I explained that I wasn't going to another company. I didn't want another operational role. I wanted to focus on writing and speaking because the COVID-19 crisis reminded me that our time here is not a guarantee. We must seize the moment, and pursue our passions.

After my departure, I went through an identity crisis. *Paul Wolfe, author, advisor, speaker...* What does that mean?! I am selling myself and what I have to say.

Being tied to corporate America for over three decades, my identity had become largely made up of the roles I held. I had spent the last eight years helping to grow a company from one thousand to over eleven thousand employees and leading them through the pandemic. Two or three months into the pandemic, in what already felt like my five hundredth Zoom meeting, I was listening to employees share their quarantine experiences and concerns. I realized a fundamental truth from the pandemic and all it had wrought: everyone is a human being first. We as HR leaders, and leaders in general, think of people as employees. *The accountant. The manager. The salesperson.* However, we share a lot more in common than we may think at first glance.

One thing that makes us the same is the fulfillment of our physiological needs for human survival: air, food, drink, shelter, clothing, warmth, and sleep. If these needs are not satisfied, the human body cannot function optimally. As study, work, and relationships fill more of our time, we add to our lives further with the needs of safety, love and belongingness, and esteem. We also have cognitive needs, aesthetic needs, the need for self-actualization, and the need for transcendence. According to psychologist Abraham Maslow, this is where our "peak experiences and personal development" take shape and dictate our motivations and behaviors.[8]

When we dismiss these elevated needs, that largely occur around the workplace, as unimportant or trivial rather than celebrating them as shared human experiences, we focus on our differences and become *more divided*. Since leaders are charged with setting the tone and context for having these needs met, their attitudes and actions are critical.

The Era of Elevated Engagement and Empowerment

Your capacity for greatness to meet the numbers and bounce high from the bottom line is honorable. However, it is minuscule compared to what you can achieve with these eight empathetic, expressive practices:

1. Align who you are as a person with who you are as a leader
2. Encourage excitement and innovation, eliminate all indifference
3. Create psychological safety
4. Have a clear mission and purpose buy-in
5. Establish unshakable bonds of trust and dedication
6. Prioritize individual, team, and enterprise-wide wellbeing
7. Protect your people-first brand from competitors
8. Amplify your position, momentum, and legacy

---

[8] Saul McLeod, "Maslow's Hierarchy of Needs," *Simple Psychology*, published 2007, updated April 04, 2022, https://www.simplypsychology.org/maslow.html.

Your greatest power lies in the ability to emote and demonstrate these feelings. This means that you are a *human*, not a grand specimen of automation, and that you are making use of the twenty-seven different emotions that you possess.[9] When you exhibit those feelings with empathetic, expressive practice, your interactions and relationships will amplify your business objectives, mission, and purpose.

Engagement is of primary importance, and not just to younger employees. I will repeat what I said about age diversity when I was interviewed on *TODAY* by financial editor and AARP contributor Jean Chatzky. "People are staying in the workforce longer. People want to be engaged. There is a place for everybody."[10]

We are all fragile, intricate beings. We exist. We have collective vulnerability. How do we navigate having a great life? It may not be rocket science, but it is a science: biology. Leading as a human being first, who is in touch with your body and those feelings-affecting chemicals, will make all the difference between your influence and your *impact*.

---

[9] Alan S. Cowen and Dacher Keltner, "Self-report captures 27 distinct categories of emotion bridged by continuous gradients," *PNAS.org*, September 5, 2017, 114 (38) E7900-E7909, https://doi.org/10.1073/pnas.1702247114.
[10] Jean Chatzky, "5 secrets of success for workers over 50," *TODAY*, November 26, 2018, https://www.today.com/money/5-secrets-success-workers-over-50-t141965.

*"Without reflection, we go blindly on our way,
creating more unintended consequences, and
failing to achieve anything useful."*

—MARGARET J. WHEATLEY,
Management Consultant

CHAPTER 1

REFLECT

Growing up in North Miami, my first role model was my mother, who taught fifth and sixth grade for thirty-two years in Carol City, Florida. She was offered higher positions in school administration, but she turned them all down because she loved teaching children in the classroom. She had her PhD and made $47,000 per year back in 1992. But why haven't all teachers earned twice as much money? No offense to professional athletes, but why are *they* the ones signing $100 million contracts? I think of my beloved mother every time educators get shorted.

I went to the University of Miami for one year on a full scholarship. I did not enjoy it, so I left. Being an educator who believed strongly in a college education, my mother freaked out. Several years later, the unthinkable happened. I was finishing my bachelor's degree at Nova Southeastern University, and while working on a marketing project with other students one night, I got a phone call. Every Thursday, my mother and her teacher friends from school would go out to dinner. On the night of November 5, 1992, my mother was about a mile and a half away from our house. An eighteen-year-old had just picked up her new car and was driving around eighty miles an hour. She lost control of her car, went through the median, and hit my mother's car head-on. They both died instantly. My mom's boyfriend called me to deliver the horrendous news.

Her death affected me in numerous ways. It has certainly informed my sense of loyalty to loved ones and my people-focused leadership style, which I exercise at home as well. I don't believe that you only lead and act empathetically in the workplace. For example, my husband was struggling with the decision to go to Ohio when his mother was ill. COVID-19 cases were soaring at the time, so much was unknown, and there were no vaccines yet available. Knowing how much she meant to him, I urged him to find a way to go. I shared with him that I would give anything if I could have even five more minutes with my mom to tell her everything that I needed and wanted to. We put a plan together. He drove to Ohio, while taking great travel and visitation precautions, to spend time with his mother during her final days in hospice care.

My mother motivated her students to be better by taking time to understand their behavioral and psychological well-being, not just their academic standing. She was sensitive to their entire being, including their relationships with other children and teachers. She knew that they could have issues happening at home and recognized that she could make a difference in their lives. However, the dance was delicate, and she couldn't get too involved. This required self-regulation, which I observed her demonstrate toward students and parents. She comprehended feelings and emotions without leaning on judgment. She was cognizant of her impact on students' very impressionable minds, as well as their learning and development.

You and I are not children; we are adult leaders. But I'm sure you feel some resonance here with my mother, her students, or both. We are all human beings first, before any other role or persona we fall into throughout our personal and professional development. All human experiences contribute to our emotional intelligence (EI). As a passionate and fiercely involved teacher at the same school for so many decades, my mother's EI was elevated.

Research published in the *American Journal of Pharmaceutical Education*[11] has proven that a strong propensity for emotional intelligence increases one's ability to make sound decisions, build and sustain collaborative relationships, deal effectively with stress, and cope with constant change. It enables an individual not only to perform well in the workplace but also to accomplish various other goals and objectives in their life. This is an influential leader.

According to Daniel Goleman, an American psychologist and author of the groundbreaking book, *Emotional Intelligence*, EI has five key elements that, when managed, help leaders attain a higher level of emotional intelligence.

1. *Self-awareness,* recognizing the effect your actions, moods, and emotions have on other people

---

[11] Romanelli F, Cain J, Smith KM. Emotional intelligence as a predictor of academic and/or professional success. Am J Pharm Educ. June 15, 2006, https://www.ncbi.nlm.nih.gov/pmc/articles/PMC1636947/.

2. *Self-regulation*, waiting for the right time and place to express emotions (Those who are skilled in self-regulation tend to be flexible and adapt well to change. They are also good at managing conflict and diffusing tense or difficult situations.)

3. *Motivation,* by things beyond external rewards like fame, money, recognition, and acclaim (They have a passion to fulfill their own inner needs and goals. They seek internal rewards, get into flow states when engrossed in an activity, and pursue peak performance.)

4. *Empathy* toward how others are feeling, which also informs your responses to people

5. *Social skills*, including active listening, verbal communication skills, nonverbal communication skills, leadership, and persuasiveness[12]

What I love most about Daniel Goleman's philosophy is best stated in this quote:

> *The best news is that 'emotional literacy' is not fixed early in life. Every parent, every teacher, every business leader, and everyone interested in a more civilized society has a stake in this compelling vision of human possibility.*

I like to think of the five key elements of emotional intelligence like this—know and manage yourself, show emotions, and hone your social skills. We are all capable of this because we are all human beings.

---

[12] Daniel Goleman, *Emotional Intelligence,* New York, New York: Random House Publishing, 2005.

Emotional Literacy is Internal Power to Source for Hard Decisions

As I reflect on my time at tech companies, I know that I was a part of something constantly growing. Innovation reigned, which contributed to my growth as a human being and leader. When we reflect more, we repress less. We gain perspective. We expand. It's like the information stays closer to the surface, easier to access. Conversely, if we barrel through the days without reflection, a kind of dullness and stagnancy materializes. Then, all this time has passed, sometimes faster than we realize. Did we experience that? How did we feel about it? What did we learn? Did we change?

When you reflect on a situation, experience, or feeling, you relive it in an emotionally intelligent way. You might not repeat mistakes if you notice the patterns that tend to show up. Learnings set in. You may do better next time. Lessons in life, and leadership, add to your education and your training. In being more empathetic and expressive through this enrichment, you're taking time to recognize a meaningful process you're permitting for yourself. Improved emotional intelligence will inevitably improve your self-construct, as well as your overall leadership skills.

AN EMPATHETIC, EXPRESSIVE LEADER'S PLAYBOOK
Don't Let the Shifts Make You Bitter—Be Better
Ekta Vyas, PhD

Ekta Vyas is the Chief Human Resources Officer at Keck Medicine of the University of Southern California, as well as an adjunct management faculty member with San Jose State University's College and Graduate School of Business.

Her background includes twenty-eight years of progressive consulting and leadership experience in human resources strategy and operations, spanning across the continuum of multiple human resources functions. She is a frequent keynote and panel speaker, a *Forbes* Influencer, and a featured author for the book, *Mission Matters: World's Leading Entrepreneurs Reveal Their Top Tips to Success*. She is a certified Strategic HR Practitioner from Cornell, a Strategic Human Resources Business Partner, a Human Capital Strategist, a Society for Human Resource Management-Senior Certified Professional, a certified emotional intelligence and personal brand assessor, as well as a coach. In her own words below, Ekta talks about the radical leadership shifts that have occurred over the past few years and how to be better for them.

Leaders, culture begins with you
Culture is one of the most complex phenomena in organizations. It's quite an abstract thing. Edgar Schein[13] refers to it as an empirically based abstraction. It's not something tangible you can touch, but you experience it as you go through the organization, and it takes years to evolve. It keeps evolving on a regular basis. Every time a new leader joins, they establish how they're going to lead the organization. One year or two

---

[13] Edgar H. Schein, *Organizational Culture and Leadership*, Somerset, New Jersey: Wiley, 2010.

years down the road, the way they have led the organization shifts the culture. There's a lot of evolution, and that is how cultures are formed and made.

Now, there will always be an underpinning of who we are as an organization based on its foundational elements and identity, the industry, the communities you serve, and sometimes even the geography and region where your business exists. Macro-cultures will have subcultures within them, depending on how large your organization is. What kind of culture exists depends on what your organization has done in the past couple of years and, more importantly, how that was done.

Another important influence [on your organization's culture] is how it is evolving and shaping itself based on where it is going. Everyone has a different model for their business. There is no one principle that all industries or organizations are following. They're learning from *industry growth* or *devastation*. The reason I use these two terms is that they're very contrasting. In recent context, certain organizations or industries had a positive surge from the pandemic because of either return on the services they were offering, or because they were able to pivot quickly to adapt their offerings to the larger needs and shift the way they were working almost overnight. Others were hit very hard and had to adapt for survival or completely change directions. Growth in these cases was not even a consideration, as merely continued existence was the priority.

Wherever you are, the culture that exists, although invisible, will be the facilitator, enabler, and accelerator to help you get to your true north. Although, this depends on how evolved your culture is to support the strategic direction of the firm and prepare your workforce to take you where you want to go. The challenge is that it takes years for an organizational culture to form. It can't be uprooted and changed overnight when a big internal shift is needed to respond to new externalities and environmental pressures. That's where leadership matters most.

It's extremely significant for leaders to understand that they are the prime and strongest influencers on the culture of their organization. When a purposeful shift is needed in the culture of an organization, the biggest challenge or enabler is the readiness of leadership. Despite the literature and immense education about change management and leadership, there are many leaders around who are quite resistant to changing their ways of working and adapting to the needs of the time. Certainly, there are nimble ones who learn lessons quickly and understand when they need to shift how they lead and evolve their worldviews and mental models. However, there are also those that can't wait to get back to their old habits and mental models once the crisis is over. That kind of leadership is a barrier to evolving organizational culture to where it needs to be for success and where the future lies. Those are the organizations where culture eats strategy for breakfast!

Reflect and evolve
One of the biggest things that organizations need is agile, adaptive, and forward-thinking leadership. If you don't have forward-thinking leaders, and they want to go back to old mental models, that will devastate the organization because it will create a rift. In the current context, it will create a disconnect and some kind of battle with employees who have now gone through a very devastating work-life impact from the COVID-19 era. They have started reimagining how their future could look, their work-life balance, what kind of occupational field they want to be in, what kind of job they want to have, and what kind of skills they would like to obtain. They're reskilling themselves, and they're upskilling themselves. They're also questioning their employee-employer relationship from the perspective of choosing what opportunities to say yes to and which ones to turn down. Let's not forget that many have gone

through much suffering and pain, uncertainty, ambiguity, and anxiety. They cannot wait to have a better future, a more certain future—and quite rightfully. Phases of uncertainty and hopelessness create a stronger sense of what the future should look like. Thus, reflection becomes an integral part of regeneration.

If the reflection is so critical to the workforce wanting to influence and shape their future differently, it should be more important to leaders who have the power and position to leverage this opportunity. Those leaders can use the emergent workforce choices to create a competitive advantage for the business. Regardless of whether you are a forward-thinking leader or have to adapt, the choice to keep operating with a pre-pandemic mindset is a recipe for failure. Therefore, evolving yourself is a career necessity for leaders to survive and thrive. Once leaders commit to evolving themselves, they realize forward-thinking strategies that align with the primary needs of today's workforce are what will move the needle on company culture. Culture comes first, strategies come second!

If culture comes first, human beings come first since "culture is a pattern of shared tacit assumptions learned or developed by a group as it solves its problems of external adaptation and internal integration that have worked well enough to be considered valid and, therefore, to be taught to new members as the correct way to perceive, think, and feel in relation to those problems," according to Schein.

For the needs of the day, outdated assumptions need to be replaced with those newly conceived to propel tomorrow's strategies forward. It doesn't matter that you're the employer, signing off on the salary check. Today's worker will go to look for somebody who aligns with how they feel and think. That will happen sooner or later, so don't let it be a lesson learned rather than an opportunity leveraged.

Reflect to sustain as well

As stated earlier, I'm not implying you must give up on everything you've forged in the organization. There are a lot of elements within a culture that you can preserve that will help you keep moving forward. A lot of elements were strong enough to get your organization through the pandemic. I have talked to many leaders who led well during the recent crisis.

I probed, "You had to react immediately. You had to shift from where you were operating. What made you sail through the pandemic and keep going stronger?"

One of the responses I received was, "To pivot and adapt immediately, we already had a culture of collaboration since the pandemic needed a joint effort to fight on."

So, if that's the element of your culture that had you sail through the pandemic, keep that, sustain it. At the same time, identify what was pulling you back, the rigid elements in your culture, which could be a barrier going forward. Sustaining those elements is like committing both cultural and strategic suicide.

In conversations with leaders lately, I have heard a lot about innovation, whether that be adding it in or strengthening their already innovative culture. An innovative culture could have made all the difference in helping you respond before you even realized that it was an unplanned change that you managed effectively. Sustain that and you just learned about a strong element of your culture that engages your workforce.

Understand all aspects of your leadership style

Before you lead an organization, lead yourself. After you've learned to lead, evolve yourself. Of course, it's easier said than done. This gets back to the significance of emotional intelligence for a leader, as discussed by Daniel Goleman as the

"Sine Qua Non of Leadership." Today's leader-worker dynamics is asking you to find growth in how you think, growth in how you shift your worldview to adapt to what someone else's worldview is asking of you. Also, you need to make sure that you can unlearn your old mental models in order to adapt and lead effectively to bring your organization and employees into the future. It's foundational for leaders in knowing how to engage their workforce.

Being emotionally intelligent is not a new request of leaders. It was needed pre-pandemic for engagement, during the crisis, and will continue to be needed. It's a crucial skill set to be an effective leader because being emotionally intelligent means being able to understand yourself. You need to understand what is helping you be an effective leader, what is hindering you being an effective leader, and you need to work on your blind spots. Figure out what doesn't help you lead effectively, that doesn't help you create a positive perception about you, about who you are as a leader. Equally important, understand the emotions of others so you can lead them better.

To lead others better, wear your "human" hat this time around. Perhaps, that will help your brain to connect with the heart of your workforce. Remember, emotional intelligence is about balancing thinking and feeling for the desired outcome. It's about the mind and heart equally. Different times call for different requirements of a leader, so you have to keep reassessing. Allow time and space to get to know the emotions of others. Do your own temperature checks, surveys of employees, and run your own trends. Talk to those who are staying, and talk to those who are joining. As the spectrum of employee-employer relations is changing, know the changes. Could it be a marketing thing or a brand component resonating with people? Why not enhance that one? Then, maybe another trend is why people are leaving. Customize that look to your organization's realities. It's not about generalizing and industry trends. You've got to draw your own conclusions to understand your own workforce's patterns.

Being better starts with the leader

Leadership sets the tone from the top down, and this permeates throughout the organization as all leaders find themselves on the same page. If you have different strata of leadership with different worldviews on what the future looks like, it's quite unhealthy and detrimental. Leadership alignment is a necessity to keep heading towards the true north. Only then can an organization define what kind of culture and leadership competencies are needed to steer the ship forward or turn the ship around. Have one shared voice of leadership influencing your organization's culture.

Express and engage

Be transparent in your internal communication, so people can hear what you're saying. When you listen to each other and align your thinking, you clarify any confusion. You clarify the disconnect. Then you help your workforce understand what your true north is and what key elements you are instilling in your culture for it to be the force that moves you forward together.

Employees are not unreasonable as long as you help them understand why you think certain things are important to keep, embrace, or let go. If you have a justification for your vision, that can help them understand why you're asking them to get onboard with your proposed changes and strategies to move towards the model you need, they will get on board. When you don't communicate and are not transparent, they cannot see that it's in their best interest. You must have an aligned future. That is when you get your workforce to go where you are heading. In the end, you get better together so you can all keep moving forward.

Reactive mode compromises reflection

It's no one's fault with so much happening at a rapid speed. Most of us are freaking out because things seem out of control. So much control has been lost to unpredictable happenings lately. It is easy to want to regain control somehow. Don't let the need for power and control be your internal focus. Empowerment is a leader's new superpower.

Empathy, trust, and inclusion are your enablers, the crucial leadership competencies. It can feel abstract. Your people will tell you if you've been inclusive or not. It's a behavior that can be seen in your actions. It's not the type of strategy where you can check boxes and quantify it. Inclusion will be observed and seen by your people when you talk about being empathetic. When they came to you with a problem, how did you present yourself as a leader? Walk the talk. *Inclusion. Trust. Empathy.* These are heavy words, but people either see it or they don't. You cannot use words like "authenticity" if you don't meet them with actions. Reflect. Work on yourself. Understand your gaps in being today's leader. If you need help, ask for it. Seek coaching. Unlearning mental models takes time, and you're being watched all the time. You can't hide how you are as a leader. Don't let the shifts make you bitter. Instead, choose to be better.

I concur with Ekta in that there is no going back to anything from before. The way we led, the way we worked, and the way we lived pre-COVID-19 has all changed. The best companies and leaders are going to understand that, and move forward with developing the new paradigm of LIFE— where work is a part of it, just as are family, friends, hobbies, travel, etc. The culture of a company does not necessarily need to change completely, but it does have to evolve for it to embrace new ways of working and leading. Jeff Bezos was on to something when he said, "What's dangerous is not to evolve."

"Vulnerability is the birthplace of connection and the path to the feeling of worthiness. If it doesn't feel vulnerable, the sharing is probably not constructive."

—BRENÉ BROWN,
Researcher on Shame, Vulnerability, and Leadership

CHAPTER 2

SHARE

In the working world, you start sharing personal data as soon as a company or leader lands on your sunny horizon, promising you a new future. For some, it's difficult to draw boundaries around or be cautious in what they share. Their inclination is to throw everything at these new possibilities because job candidates are usually optimistic. After all, they have a lot riding on this possibility materializing into the desired outcome—like income, title, prestige, an exciting challenge, or a different space for their leadership abilities. I have been seated on both sides of this table.

If you encounter any potential warning flags during the interview process, when everyone is expected to be on their best behavior, you need to think about what you're getting yourself into. It's like dating. I always joke that dating and recruiting are similar, you just expect different outcomes. You detect flags in prospective romantic partners just as you might in prospective managers, organizations, and the cultures. Are they a fit for you? As the relationship goes further, and people get more comfortable, you could see the events those flags warned of unfold.

I tell hiring managers and candidates to walk away if they see potential flags. It's not the cynic in me, it's that I've sadly seen disasters play out. It's better when you are running toward something rather than running from something. Thoroughly examine a company's mission and what you require from them. If your financial circumstances are even slightly looser than "taking this job is a complete necessity," pause before you commit.

At my last company, all involuntary terminations came to me for approval. We had processes in place for conversations around performance and improvement plans we could implement to help employees whose performance needed a boost. The ultimate goal was to help the employee course-correct and regain strong performance. However, not every employee did improve in their role.

In one particular case, the termination request was for someone in sales. It was a quota-driven role, and we had a lot of data supporting their underperformance. The HR business partner who submitted the request shared with me that the employee truly believed in the mission of the company and, other than not being able to achieve quota, they were a great employee.

The lack of quota attainment supported the termination, but something in me said, "Is there some other role for this employee?" Because of my position, I had an overview of all the roles we were currently recruiting for. I surmised that the employee might be qualified for several of the roles. After we discussed the performance issues with the employee, I asked if any other roles interested them. They came back to me with more roles than I originally thought would suit them. They shared that their background was in customer service and felt that this department would be a better fit.

We made the change, filling one of many roles open in Client Success at the time, and that employee flourished in their new role. It only took a couple of honest conversations to place them appropriately at the company. In this case, it was important to weigh both the data side and the human side of the situation. Because everyone had honestly shared their perspectives, we were able to think outside the box and find a solution that was a win for both the company and the employee.

Another example of the significance of sharing showed up in an ongoing issue between an employee and their leader. There had been tension, disagreement, and angst between these two for a while. It was so obvious to team members and other members of the department that it had become a running joke. The employee constantly disagreed with their leader and made negative comments to other employees. Sometimes this brought other employees into their vortex of negativity. Clearly, not a positive thing for team or department morale.

Neither one had formally raised a concern with HR about the other, but there were always comments here or there that kept HR informed. I was getting a general update on this department from HR when this issue came up. I asked to be reminded of what we had done to try and make this better, and they ran through a rather lengthy list of attempts. I then asked, "Have we ever brought them in the same room with an objective third party to air their differences and see if we could make things better?"

We had been working with a coach who focused on epigenetics, the study of how your behaviors and environment can cause changes that affect the way your genes work. Based on the work this coach had already started to do in our organization, we took her advice and brought these two employees together to share their issues and concerns. Each took some persuading to show up for this conversation, but both agreed.

We set ground rules for the conversation. At first, there were short exchanges with a lot of silence in between. Then we started using open-ended questions to get them both to open up. As the conversation went on, you could almost feel the tension in the room dissipating. Now, I never thought for a moment that they were going to be friends, but I wanted to clear the air between them so they could have an amicable working relationship. Having them each share their perspectives helped them to respect each other, become more civil with each other, and helped them grow as human beings. In situations like this, if you start from the position that we are both human beings— we are more alike than different—things can improve. You only need to honestly talk and listen to one another.

Research from Michael Parke, an assistant professor of Management at Wharton, highlights the benefits of expressing emotions in the workplace. "When teams have supportive environments where members share their feelings *and* empathetically respond to each other, they can increase their ability to solve problems, elaborate information, and generate ideas," explains a *Knowledge at Wharton* article presenting Parke as a featured faculty member. This idea is illuminated in Parke's paper fittingly titled, "The Creative and Cross-Functional Benefits of Wearing Hearts on Sleeves: Authentic Affect Climate, Information Elaboration, and Team Creativity."[14]

Parke said, in the same *Knowledge at Wharton* article,

We found that teams that have this environment where they feel comfortable sharing their genuine emotions with their team members, and they don't just ignore [emotions] but they work through them, not only come up with better ideas and insights, but they also get to the richer discussions as well. They're more creative. They produce more creative outcomes.

Let's not forget that feelings are messengers of needs. It's much easier to meet a need when you're aware of it. Without open and honest communications, this cannot happen. We as a society have evolved from the thoughts and norms of the 1950s and we as leaders need to do the same. In the 1950s, leaders were asked to be imposters without emotions, not their true selves. Words like *command* and *authority* come to mind, and not in the modern way of being an authority or thought leader. Humans are intricate, fragile beings with emotions. We need to understand where those emotions are coming from and why we are having them. They can be extraordinarily useful in connecting with other humans. It is okay to say that you don't have the answer

[14] Knowledge at Wharton Staff, "All the Feels: How Companies Can Benefit from Employees' Emotions," Knowledge at Wharton, September 7, 2021, https://knowledge.wharton.upenn.edu/article/how-companies-can-benefit-from-employees-emotions/.

for everything—that you cry, sweat, and feel anxious or fearful—because that is what it means to be a human being!

Naked, But Not Afraid: Courageous Vulnerability

Two survivalists meet for the first time, nude, and are given the task of surviving a stay in the wilderness for twenty-one days. Each survivalist is allowed to bring one helpful item, such as a machete or a fire starter. After they meet in the assigned locale, the partners must build a shelter and find water and food. This is *Naked and Afraid*, which has aired for fourteen seasons. One episode I saw took place in Brazil. The contestants had to make impossible decisions, like whether to get to a location by swimming in tiger shark-infested waters or by going underground through a cave system, all the while suffering from exhaustion, dehydration, malnourishment, bug bites, and who knows what else. The environment—at least when the contestants arrive—is breathtakingly gorgeous, but with each day, increasingly dangerous. This may be great TV while snacking and lounging as a non-survivalist, but I *felt* their acute exposure, their vulnerability. Twenty-one days of this raw susceptibility to life-threatening harm—they have every right to be AFRAID!

Many of the situations we face as leaders are vulnerability-lite, in comparison. At least you can turn back or escape. But if you stick to it, you understand what it feels like on the other side of that scary situation and you push through—it's immeasurably rewarding. Vulnerability is scary, and it exposes us. It is the most powerful tool one can use to shift a relationship.

A friend and colleague once shared a story with me about vulnerability. He was hired to manage an existing team that had worked already together for several years. Most of the team was supportive, but he knew that some of them had doubts about him as a leader. He decided to show a more vulnerable and human side of himself to gain the acceptance and support of the department.

The company sponsored softball teams, where departments played against one another. It was a great after-work release and team-building program. My friend was, well, not particularly athletic. The thought of playing on the department softball team brought back childhood anxiety and stress. Rather than turning down a spot on the team and alienating employees, he decided to use it to his advantage. To avoid complete humiliation and make his insecurities work in his favor, he shared with the team that his athletic abilities were sorely lacking, but in support of the department, he agreed to play and would give it his best effort.

His performance on the field was predictable. However, in being upfront about his lack of athletic prowess and owning it, he showed a human side that the team was not used to in a leader. They appreciated it. It humanized him. They still teased him, but unlike in childhood, this time he was in on it, and he enjoyed the interactions his bad playing inspired. Sharing and vulnerability brought his team together. They didn't win the championship, but he and the team benefitted from the shared experiences and improved connections.

In 2020, I was vulnerable with eleven thousand employees shortly after we all shifted to working remotely because of the pandemic. We started a weekly Q&A session along with a weekly email. I wrote about what was going on, decisions we were making, and new programs we were rolling out to support our employees.

I decided I was ready to share my struggle with OCD (obsessive-compulsive disorder, which is a chronic anxiety disorder). I hear these letters get tossed around casually when labeling (or judging) others' behavior, but let's consider what it means in a clinical sense: "The cycle of OCD persists through operant conditioning, where compulsions are behavioral responses that reduce anxiety. The effectiveness of the compulsion is what negatively reinforces that behavior in response to obsessions," according to Dr. Menije Boduryan-Turner. She explains that having OCD "greatly affects a person's life due to intrusive thoughts, anxiety, and uncertainty. OCD obsessions are intrusive and can be triggered at any time."[15]

According to the Anxiety and Depression Association of America, approximately 2.3 percent of the population has OCD, which is about 1 in 40 adults and 1 in 100 children in the U.S., so you never know who may be going through this experience. I was diagnosed several years before the pandemic and had been managing it well until then. But at that point, my OCD began to manifest itself in different ways. The medications I was on and the behavioral therapies I had been taught were no longer working.

The internal communications manager, who I worked with on my weekly emails, sent me a draft and as usual, I made a few tweaks. But this time, I added two paragraphs of my own that described what I was going through. I sent the marked-up document back to her.

A few minutes later, she sent me a message in Slack, our shared online workspace, and said, "Are you sure you want

---

[15] Single Care Team, "OCD statistics 2022," *The Checkup Blog*, February 15, 2022, https://www.singlecare.com/blog/news/ocd-statistics/.

to include the paragraphs that you added?" I sat back and thought for a moment, asking myself, *is there any reason I should not share this?* The answer was no, so I told her to hit send. It was liberating. "This is me!" Looking back on it now, at that moment, I wanted employees to know the real me. I was about to discover that there is power in that.

My email went out as usual on Thursday morning with my additional paragraphs, and I went about my typical workday. Later that afternoon, I had a break between Zoom meetings, so I got a chance to catch up on emails. Within that short window, I had gotten about four hundred or so new emails. More than usual, needless to say! I started to scroll through them. Most of them were from employees showing support. Some employees shared that they had OCD as well and how they were managing during the pandemic. Others shared that they had other mental health issues. A lot of employees shared their appreciation and were surprised that an executive would share such personal information.

When I first started to learn about diversity and inclusion, I would say, "Here is the way I think about people. We are all books, and we each have many chapters. These chapters make us who we are." There are things in our life that have shaped the way we think about something, or how we are hard-wired, or why we have a certain reaction to something. It's not until you open the book and read those chapters that you understand why someone thinks or behaves as they do. This can help explain why they may have a visceral reaction to a word, phrase, or action. When someone shares, seek to understand and empathize with what they have said. "Be curious, not judgmental." (I love that quote, which has been attributed to several people.) Those are words we should all live by.

I am a book, and I have an OCD chapter. Changing life circumstances sent it out of control for a bit. It is better now. The emotional part of me as a leader is not absent. The day after my email disclosing my struggles with my OCD and anxiety was sent, I was in a Zoom meeting, and an employee said, "I just want to start by saying 'thank you.'"

I must have looked perplexed because she said to me, "You have no idea what you did, do you?"

I said, "No."

She responded with, "You made a lot of us realize that executives are just like us."

It was then that I realized the true power of vulnerability. No company or team can function at its highest capacity without vulnerable leaders.

So, now you know *Paul*; you have had a peek at a chapter in my book. If I am having a bad day or act in an unusual manner, perhaps you will understand what is going on, and remember that I am human, too. What a powerful tool. Demonstrating who you are and receiving affirming feedback.

AN EMPATHETIC, EXPRESSIVE LEADER'S PLAYBOOK
Sharing Stories and Hot Buttons from Day One
Irina Soriano

Irina Soriano is a TEDx speaker and the author of *Generation Brand*, a modern playbook for cultivating our *life-brand*, the evolution of our lives and reputation online since birth. She currently serves as vice president at a tech company and is a sought-after keynote speaker. Irina's passion for enabling others to control their life-brand, coupled with her career spanning Europe, the Middle East, Africa, Asia-Pacific, and the U.S., allows her to deliver an inspiring message to individuals. Her talks teach audiences how to actively build a compelling life-brand to unleash their full career potential, while powerfully representing their company and its brand value.

Irina has a particularly strong passion for supporting women and enabling gender equity in business. Through her work, her goal is to inspire women in all career stages. She wants them to take action and make a significant contribution to gender parity through their career advancement, inspiring other women to follow their lead. In Irina's own words below, she shares the benefits of demonstrating vulnerability as a leader.

Share your story, build trust, and get superlative results
I've led teams of over fifty people. No matter how small or large my team is, my goal is to always build personal connections with everyone on my team quickly. Not just my direct reports. I consider vulnerability to be a key ingredient for great leadership. I was lucky to learn from many of my bosses how it can change a working relationship, creating deep trust. When people join my team, I spend time sharing my personal story with them. That includes career milestones, but it focuses more on the rest of my life. Relationships I fostered, health and personal challenges I had to overcome, and experiences I made

when living and working all over the world. Often, people get surprised to hear about obstacles I had to overcome, but it opens a door. I let them in on my life and allow them to see what is behind the face they see every day at work. Many decide to share their personal stories after hearing my own.

The other piece I share with people is what I coin my "hot buttons" or phrases that trigger me—such as low-quality standards, for instance. I have a high expectation of myself and the people that work for me. Some hot buttons are not obvious, so by creating visibility around them employees will understand what I care about. We all have triggers. Revealing them early allows people to interpret certain reactions better, and it lets me refer back to them at any point in time.

Sharing gives unbridled freedom to express
Social media culture has changed in the last two years and people are opening up more and more about personal stories, experiences, and challenges online. That vulnerability can be an example for others. They can learn and grow through someone else's story, and they can see that even senior executives are people—just like them.

Being authentic at work and in public settings (such as social media) changes the game. The average person spends about ninety thousand hours at work throughout their lifetime. Not being yourself, "wearing a mask," and hiding your true personality might feel necessary at times, but it is ultimately a career blocker rather than a career driver. The key is to find an organization and leaders that value our personality, and not every organization is always a fit.

Especially for women in leadership positions, authenticity and sharing work and life challenges with the next generation embarking on their professional journey can create a paradigm shift. Women need to be role models, as there are still far too few women in leadership. We carry a responsibility to give back and to support the women that will step into our footsteps in the years ahead.

Authenticity requires transparency

People often want to maintain a certain image; that is human nature. We do not tend to lead with our weaknesses and challenges, but with the areas we shine in. Becoming more authentic is a process—it requires courage. There is a fear of being judged by others that flows with the process of being an authentic leader. It's the same in business, we have to be honest and look at where we can improve, where we have gaps, and what we're not doing that we should be doing. That can be painful at times.

Personally, I struggled to be authentic in my early career. I held back and didn't show myself fully until I received feedback from one of my managers. They said that the challenges in my life, the struggles, and the obstacles are actually the things that other people connect with, because they likely can relate in some form or another. Creating a bond through commonality is one of the most powerful ways to build relationships at work and in life.

Feedback is liberating

I have always treated feedback as a gift, positive or constructive. That sounds obvious, yet people generally do not feel comfortable giving or receiving feedback. The giver might think that feelings could get hurt or the feedback may not resonate, and they might hit a defensive wall. The taker might feel discouraged or lose confidence in their abilities. Yet, these are stories that we tell ourselves. When organizations foster a culture of feedback across all levels, sharing areas to improve and continue becomes a normal part of everyone's work environment. It is perceived as a tool for accelerated professional and personal development. It is seen as a gift. It is equally important to learn how to deliver quality feedback.

A few steps I teach people I work with:

- Start by describing the specific situation your feedback relates to. What happened, when did it happen, and who was present? The key is to share what you observed, not what others told you (then they should deliver the feedback).
- Go on by sharing how what happened made you feel. Describe how it might impact co-workers, the company, and even customers. This part makes the feedback more relatable.
- Lastly, suggest how things can be improved (constructive feedback) or reinforced (positive feedback) to an agreeable outcome together.

With her teachings, Irina epitomizes evolution to me. We, as leaders, have been taught and programmed to behave a certain way. In this, I believe we have done ourselves a disservice—by hiding who we really are. You must be self-aware, knowing what is appropriate to share, and knowing when to share it. There will often be someone else experiencing a similar situation, struggle or success, and sharing your story can be amazing. You will inspire others to be more vulnerable, open, and empathetic. As leaders, we have a responsibility to encourage and allow more people to be seen and heard.

"Empathy is about standing in someone else's shoes, feeling with his or her heart, seeing with his or her eyes. Not only is empathy hard to outsource and automate, but it makes the world a better place."

—DANIEL H. PINK,
Thought Leader on Business, Work, Creativity, and Behavior

CHAPTER 3

SEE

Seeing is believing, right? In business, we have to predict, analyze, benchmark, measure, and inspire. I would argue that seeing is the first step of the process—that is, seeing the human beings behind the process. We are seeing and being seen every step of the way.

Before the decision was made for all our employees to work from home at the beginning of the COVID-19 pandemic, we had to reflect and assess. Will everyone be productive from home? How will performance and morale be affected? Do all employees possess the necessary equipment? Can our tech sustain eleven thousand remote employees at once? We were still in that box of everyone reporting to a physical office, and it was difficult to answer these questions. However, we would soon find the answers.

On March 2, 2020, the senior leadership team reached a consensus. We informed our employees that beginning the following day, we would be working from home until further notice. We were the first big tech company to go all in with work-from-home (WFH). Facebook and others followed over the next week. We went into the pandemic WFH model, thinking it would last for three or four weeks. When it went on another month beyond that, we thought—*Okay, now who knows how long this will be?!*

In May, I had another moment of clarity during a Zoom meeting. I realized that we were literally and figuratively seeing a bit into everyone's personal lives. Whether it be their physical home environment—books on their shelves, art and décor—or a glimpse into their relationships at home—partners, children, parents, roommates, pets—we were all seeing much more of each other than we had before. Suddenly, it was all out there. We were broadcasting it. I held many meetings with one or more of my three dogs present, which opened up great conversations and built rapport. By seeing each other in our personalized environments, we developed better insight as to who our colleagues are as well-rounded humans. Being welcomed into one another's homes, even virtually, allowed us to learn much more than seeing a few framed photos on an office desk.

To address some of our facility concerns, we initiated a program for employees to upgrade their home offices. Mostly this stipend was used for equipment: comfortable office chairs, better audio-visual technology, and the ubiquitous ring lights. Additionally, many people upgraded or enhanced their physical environment. No longer were we able to simply present ourselves via a smart outfit worn to the office (although, Zoom meetings did allow for more casual attire below the camera).

Now, our colleagues were being invited into our personal space; our home offices, our dining rooms, or even our bedrooms. Many people used this stipend as an opportunity to improve the space their colleagues were seeing on a daily basis.

I, too, participated in the home office upgrade. I carefully curated objects, photos, and art that projected how I wished to be seen and perceived. An entire brand sprang forth from a Twitter account, @ratemyskyperoom (now a book, *How to Zoom Your Room: Room Rater's Ultimate Style Guide*, by Claude Taylor and Jessie Bahrey). Room Rater judged and suggested improvements to physical WFH environments so we could better influence how we were being seen.

As HR professionals, we tend to think about employees as, well, simply employees. That is harder to do when you are virtually present in their space. Participating in WFH Zoom meetings demonstrated that we are all human beings first, and "employee" is just one role of many. It's important to see that we all have our own unique circumstances, relationships, and life experiences.

Conversations around mental health are normal now because of the pandemic. So many people struggled with depression, grief, paranoia, and stress. Like most people, while I was performing my job, I had other issues and situations I was grappling with. As human beings first, we must make the effort to see the full human being in others. They are not only an employee, not only their job or title. We must see both what they present to us and what they do not, taking in what we observe. I learned to assume positive intent instead of taking things personally. We're all the same inside, and we're all dealing with *something else*. See the full human being. That is how we can have authentic interactions.

If I could, I would reproduce the entire "Embracing Authenticity" chapter from the book, *Arrive and Thrive: 7 Impactful Practices for Women Navigating Leadership*. It perfectly conveys what I'm trying to say here about how seeing each other clearly leads to empathetic, expressive leadership. However, this excerpt by co-author Janet Foutty, Executive Chair of the Board for Deloitte U.S., speaks enough truth to power on the subject.

Both men and women have to remain sensitive to levels of professionalism as it relates to authenticity in the workplace. We have seen women less comfortable being authentic, and less willing to share the things they have grappled with personally and professionally. This has been true for us at times in our careers as well. The willingness to share ourselves in contextually appropriate and honest ways is so important for building followership and building the next generation of leaders. In a survey Deloitte conducted on 'covering'—a term coined in 1963 to describe how individuals with identities that are known to be stigmatized made a great effort to keep the stigma from looming large—countless respondents noted the impact that authenticity from an organization's top levels could have on their own openness and honesty. As one respondent put it, 'Leaders have to uncover first. If they don't, we won't.'[16]

Later in *Arrive and Thrive*, Foutty goes on to describe a feel-good holiday story that took place in her backyard and the reaction

---

[16] Susan MacKenty Brady, Janet Foutty, and Lynn Perry Wooten. *Arrive and Thrive*, New York, New York: McGraw Hill, April 12, 2022.

from her team when she shared it. One winter, she and her family created a DIY ice skating rink, so her kids (who were eight at the time) and other family members could skate and play hockey. Her colleague, who was in attendance, snapped pictures and encouraged her to share them in her customary three-minute message with her team. That week, she opened her message with the skating rink narrative and pictures to create intimacy with this large group of people.

I painted the picture of kids skating in the backyard and how that created a very different family dynamic. We as parents appreciated our children's enthusiasm for Chicago winters; they appreciated us as parents for pursuing such an out-of-the-box experience. It was quite analogous to what we as a team were trying to achieve with our client. It was so easy, so noncontroversial, and to this day, people ask me about my skating rink and remember that message with such clarity. It made me human. It made me connected to something familiar. And when we get to know each other on a personal level better, it can make for higher-performing teams because you are more invested in each other to enable better collaboration and teamwork.

Foutty allowed another side of her to be seen, letting people see her as an entire human being. The holidays are supposed to be warm and joyful. I am curious what her openness elicited from other leaders. Did they all begin sharing scenes from their winter holidays? I wonder what conversations ensued and what kind of positive rituals may have started with her concerted action.

It's Your Job to See—Will You Sharpen Your Focus?

It is equally important for us to see others as it is for us to be seen. Who's in a meeting and not saying anything? How can you make them feel safe and let them know they will be seen and heard? How can you get them to voice their concerns and opinions? What cues may you be missing that something is amiss?

Staring at expressive faces on a screen over and over again confirmed my long-held belief that we are all more similar than different. We deal with varying circumstances, and we deal with them each in our own ways. When you're not in a headspace of empathy and vulnerability, you may feel disconnected. When you are in that space, watch how your interactions light up with engagement and empowerment.

You need to communicate vulnerable content. Share a personal story, a hot take, or give feedback in an environment where it is not going to be held against you. Not all environments are safe. How do you discern? Science and business journalist Shane Snow advocates that psychological safety is a commitment to treating each other "charitably" in both directions, which allows for the following seven favorable scenarios, as delineated in a May 2020 *Forbes* article:

1. If you make a mistake, it won't be held against you.
2. If something is wrong, you can bring it up without it being used against you.
3. It won't matter where ideas come from as long as they help the team.
4. If you need help, you can ask for it without people being shitty about it.

5. When you change your mind, people will applaud your intellectual humility rather than use it against you.
6. When you make a decision, you'll weigh what's going to be the best for the whole team—and the individuals on it—over what's best for you.
7. You'll interpret other people's actions in the best light, too.[17]

My speaking coach, Erin Weed, helps individuals discover their *why*. In essence, one's *why* is their operating system, what drives them. My *why* is *better* because I am driven by finding ways to make things better. My goals are multipronged. How can I make conditions or situations better? Better for the employees? Better for leaders? Better for the company? Better for the world? It was not a surprise that the "better" emerged from my discussions with Erin. In HR and customer service, the core of what we do is making an experience better for customers and employees.

I want to make sure people are seen and for them to see how they can be better. Therefore, when a young recruiting coordinator approached me looking for career advice, I couldn't resist making things better for her. She said to me one day, "I would like to know what a day in your life is like." Being earlier in her career, she needed encouragement and knowledge. I wanted to help her.

I replied, "Shadow me."

She was intrigued. I warned her that sometimes my job was not very exciting. We agreed on a day when we would both be in the New York City office, and she spent it shadowing me.

---

[17] Shane Snow, "How Psychological Safety Actually Works," *Forbes*, May 4, 2020, https://www.forbes.com/sites/shanesnow/2020/05/04/how-psychological-safety-actually-works/.

She was inquisitive, insightful, and I enjoyed the great conversations we had that day.

Three or four weeks later, her leader was in the New York City office with me. She said, "Whatever you did or said when Sinclair shadowed you, she will never leave this company! She is telling everyone about how you took the time to allow her to shadow you, ask questions of you, and learn more about what it means to run HR for a large company."

In 2018, I was working out of our Toronto office the week leading up to the annual Pride parade. Their senior sales leader asked me if I would participate in a fireside Q&A she was hosting, and I told her I would be happy to. During that Q&A, she asked me to tell my "coming out" story. I shared my story with the employees. It brought back some nerves, but also some great memories.

The next morning as we were waiting for the parade to begin, an employee I knew came up and asked if she could hug me. After the warm embrace, I smiled and asked her why. She started to tear up as she told me her story. She had been struggling for the last few months with how to tell her mother and sisters that she is bisexual.

After hearing me tell my story at the office Q&A, she summoned the courage to tell her family that morning at breakfast before the march. I hugged her again and asked how the conversation went. She said it went well. One of her sisters had already figured it out, and her mom had some questions, but they were all supportive. She shared that she felt relaxed, like a weight had been lifted from her shoulders.

We all want to feel seen. We all want to see others for who they truly are. We all want to be better. We're all human beings.

AN EMPATHETIC, EXPRESSIVE LEADER'S PLAYBOOK
Seeing People Is Fundamental to Developing People
Nolan Farris

Nolan Farris has been with Indeed for fourteen years and was with Yahoo! HotJobs for eight years before that. He started in sales management and his last job was running the national accounts, Fortune 1000 sales team, and focusing on selling for HR. He has spent a lot of time with leaders at all levels.

Nolan was recruited away from Yahoo! to move up to Connecticut and take on a team of fifteen salespeople at Indeed. He was employee #58, and the business made about $11 million that year. Over the next four years, Nolan helped scale Indeed significantly and added offices across the U.S.; Europe, the Middle East, and Africa; and Asia-Pacific. Indeed was acquired by Recruit four years into his tenure for over $1 billion. Here's Nolan in his own words, spotlighting his tips for seeing and developing people, which he believes contributed to his success.

Take pride in being an individual contributor
Maintain transformation continually to ensure you are looking within and continuing to wake up better than you were before. We don't spend a lot of time looking back. Maybe we don't enjoy the climb as much as we could along the way, but there are just so many future things to grow and build!

Have the courage to reflect, reinvent yourself, and boldly accept that what got you here won't get you there. Initially, our company was focusing on a couple of things—most importantly, maximizing productivity so the marketplace thought we were five times the size we were. We were obsessed with delivering a consistent message in the marketplace. Educating clients in the industry on pay-per-click advertising was very different than what they were using at Monster, Dice, or CareerBuilder.

Our job was a good balance of educating the marketplace on the future and being aggressive about growing revenue. As we started growing internationally, we had to understand each market and the appropriate message for each unique audience. It was also important to invest in leadership, as we scaled and grew our teams. We also learned very early that we wouldn't have stellar managers without significant investment of time and resources.

Invest in people

My sales coach and I built a coaching model focused on communication between an individual and manager—here is how a 1:1 meeting should be built:

1. Prepare for meetings
2. Review expectations vs. performance
3. Set measurable goals and action steps
4. Listen
5. Offer insight

At the time, what we really needed was Management 101. A lot of organizations look at training and development as a cost. When you're on this aggressive road to profitability, you lose sight of investing in people. The goal of a manager is to ensure the yellow brick road of success is clear for employees, whether that's managing them through difficult situations internally or helping them get through a deal with a client. That manager is supposed to clear that path for personal and professional success and development.

Health and family first

Big companies don't become big companies all by themselves. It takes a lot of hard work and tough decisions. Oftentimes, people are at the crossroads of those decisions. Building clarity and transparency into your culture is important, and their lives get easier if they know exactly what is expected of them for nine hours a day. When they do that well, they can go live their real life! I don't believe we live to work, as health and family absolutely must come first. You can't be good in the field or in front of a client unless you are good in your mind and heart. I think employers have a huge role to play in helping people find that healthy balance, as well as instilling confidence.

Advocate for the human being

Early on, we didn't have the same amazing benefits we do now. I can remember a colleague coming back to work after four weeks of primary caregiver leave, and her child was born premature. Even ten years ago, that seemed challenging, and it makes you realize how important great benefits are. You can transform a culture and a workplace by providing world-class benefits and flexibility within them. Behind those benefits are so many stories of ways people gained the ability to provide for their family. I think it is important to acknowledge that we built a successful company, had the ability to invest in amazing benefits, as well as a wonderful, flexible culture that could afford these great innovations! At other companies, they may not have had the opportunity. HR has been at the forefront of our benefits and care. They were fighting for people to feel good about where they work every day; a place where they are protected and taken care of.

People, not policies

Maintain a general attitude about how you treat people. The first time Paul presented to Indeed in a quarterly call, he said, "I don't believe in policies. Policies suck. If you treat your people like adults, you will get a group of adults."

The leaders' jaws dropped, but his message helped us to think about what kind of company we wanted to be. Paul backed up his message through his team and how they were managed. There was a general attitude that you needed to carry in all your conversations. This afforded the view that no one is better than the next person. Our CEO would be in a conference room and a meeting would end. A group of people would poke their heads inside and say, "We have this room reserved!" The CEO would apologize and quickly leave the room. I told him never to change this thing about Indeed.

Constant communication helps everyone be seen

During the onset of the pandemic, no one questioned sending all our people home with power cords. No one knew if it would be two weeks or six, but no one thought it would be two years. It was a constant task to keep people prepared and updated with the advice we were getting from medical experts; when people could come in and get their belongings from the office, what benefits could help with their homeschooling efforts and their mental health. It placed a continuous pressure on the HR and entire leadership team.

We did weekly calls and Paul took questions, which could get brutal at times. Such as, "Hey, I'm used to going into the office, and I'm in Texas with high energy costs at home. Are you going to pay these bills?" It got crazy many times. We did offer a stipend they could use for whatever they needed. Yet, we had to answer this same question over and over again. The constant communication with the employee base was really impressive. I think there was a very important lesson we all learned in the early days of the pandemic. Everyone has their own shit going on, and it is okay to not be okay.

Managing inclusively

We want everyone to get the same attention, whether they are working virtually or in the office. Managers need to know they can be effective virtually. That balance is more than training in facilities, tech, and accessibility. It's the vocabulary leaders use and how they communicate these things. Make sure that meetings are run from an inclusive position. "Are there questions from those of you at home?" This is managing an inclusive workplace. Continue to work in ERGs (employee resource groups) and make sure teams represent the community well. Make sure the leadership you have in place looks like the young talent you're bringing in. Always be mindful of people's varying experiences, and invest in creating an inclusive workplace where everyone can thrive. This requires open eyes and open ears. This work is meaningful and matters.

In my opinion, Nolan is the epitome of an amazing leader. He has people on his team who have been with him for years, people that will walk through fire for him. Probably most importantly, he has people that deeply respect and admire him. He sees his employees as whole human beings, and he shows up as a whole human being himself. This authenticity creates an environment of psychological safety in which his employees excel and thrive.

"The world is never quiet, even its silence eternally resounds with the same notes, in vibrations which escape our ears. As for those that we perceive, they carry sounds to us, occasionally a chord, never a melody."

—ALBERT CAMUS,
Nobel Prize in Literature Recipient

CHAPTER 4

During the pandemic, people were still working, but *where* they were working looked a bit different. You have some remote people working ten feet from their bed, some are going to a shared community space a couple of times a week, and others working on a patio overlooking the ocean. They are not all showing up to the same office every day, but they all still need to communicate with their coworkers and leaders. However, with all of the distractions in their new remote environments, how do you ensure everyone is listening when they are all logging onto Zoom from somewhere different?

Leadership consultant Deborah Grayson Riegel explains how to be a great listener in remote meetings for *Inc.*

Whether you're connecting with your colleagues over the phone or by video, being able to replicate the interpersonal connection of an in-person meeting is hard. We're often missing the clues and cues that each of us send (consciously or unconsciously) to demonstrate engagement, attention, agreement, disagreement, commitment, disinterest, and more. However, we don't have to miss them. And we shouldn't. By being an attentive active listener in remote meetings, you can not only 'read the room' (virtually speaking, of course), but you can also create an environment where your colleagues feel heard, understood, valued, and like they want to contribute to the conversation.[18]

I know that, because of how connected our world is, there is often the yearning to look at your phone, tablet, or computer in a meeting. However, I think it is more important now than ever that we are laser-focused on the meetings we are in and the people we are meeting with.

Riegel's excellent advice got me thinking about the companies I've worked in, how listening may or may not have been promoted, and the impact that had on me. How would I describe the benefits of those work environments where I've felt heard, understood? Respect, enhanced relationships, mutual trust, resolution, and a state of calm come to mind. There are a lot of solid benefits gained from being able to communicate with someone who is an effective listener.

Here are two work scenarios. Think about how the tone of each makes you feel? Then determine which company you would want a permanent desk at based on your values and goals.

---

[18] Deborah Grayson Riegel, "How to be a great listener in remote meetings," *Inc.*, May 18, 2020, https://www.inc.com/deborah-grayson-riegel/how-to-be-a-great-listener-in-remote-meetings.html.

Preface: Both companies are exceptional for different reasons. However, in the context of listening and exchanging feedback, they were very different in my personal experience.

I worked at Condé Nast from 2012 to 2014. At that time, it was a heavy print business, but the onslaught of digital was disrupting their storied business model. Condé Nast was made up of eighteen magazines, almost run like eighteen entirely different businesses. The CEO was S.I. Newhouse Jr. You would see him sitting with Anna Wintour or Graydon Carter, legendary editors in the Frank Gehry-designed cafeteria. My office was next to the Vice President of Strategy and Planning. She and I became friends, and we would confide in each other. I didn't understand how so much money was being spent on what I considered extravagant things. She said, "They think of Condé as a piece of art that grows in value over time." This helped me understand the culture a bit better.

I learned a lot while I was at Condé and met some truly amazing people. They treated VPs well, and I was one of those eighty people. But the culture didn't show as much care for all of the other employees. There existed a professional caste system, if you will, where the more senior members were treated better.

But that is not the way I think. We're all equal human beings with blood flowing through our veins. We each have our own personalities, emotions, and dreams. Therefore, I decided to act differently. Early in my time there, while leaving one evening for Grand Central Terminal, my elevator stopped on the *Vogue* floor. Anna Wintour stepped on, and I did not remain quiet and avert my eyes, as I had been advised. I held my head high, smiled, and said, "Good evening."

Of all the companies I have worked for, Indeed is the strongest example of a great company culture. The culture was driven by the mission statement: "We help people get jobs." I believe in mission-driven companies. The mission was so clear and simple; everyone understood how their role tied back to helping people get jobs. That mission is very people-oriented. Any time you asked for one word that described Indeed's culture, it was "friendly." It kept coming up. It's not like everyone is "friends," but "Indeedians" always want to help.

Here is a simple example: I was in the Dublin office for a week of work. I happened to be in a conference room. As the day turned into evening and people were leaving for the night, they kept popping their heads in to inform me I couldn't go out the front door. I needed to use a different exit. They wanted to help.

So, those are our two work scenarios, Condé Nast and Indeed. Again, both companies afforded me infinite experiences and possibilities for my next life stage. However, you can see that the two presentations of culture did not equally allow for attentive listening to others—or, I would even argue, listening to yourself.

When I was working for a large technology company, I happened to be in one of our more prominent offices for a week of meetings. I had a packed schedule. It was the cram-as-much-in-as-you-can-in-a-few-days type-schedule, so I could fly home on Friday. One evening at about 6 pm, I was about to leave for the day when I saw an employee in a conference room who I had heard of but had not met yet. She appeared to be angry. As I was walking past, I decided to pop my head in to introduce myself.

I also wanted to see if she was okay or if she needed something. When I opened the door, she immediately said, "Oh, Paul, I have been waiting for you." I was rather perplexed, and asked her why.

She replied, "I have been waiting for someone to get here to run HR, because no one seems to care about under-represented employees."

I sat down and asked her to tell me what was going on. Over about two and a half hours, she said everything she had ever wanted to say; with anger, laughter, tears, and a clear passion for who she was. She happened to be a transgender employee, and I let her share her story as I made notes along the way. I listened to her emotions, pain, and pride. We ended the evening walking to the parking garage together, where she apologized for "taking so much of my time." My response was, "It was well worth it."

Over the next few years, we would run into each other on our office travels or Slack each other just to check in. I would often ask to get her perspective on things, which was always valuable. Over this time, we grew to respect each other, care about each other, and make the company a better place together. She really had been waiting for someone to listen to what she was going through and work with her to make it better.

Listening is Automatic Support

In the spring of 2020, I had been working on talent review and succession planning programming for our senior leadership team off-site. Needless to say, the pandemic had other plans for that off-site meeting. When it became clear that we were going to be working remotely for more than just a few weeks, I decided we needed to pivot our programming to something that would help with what we were all experiencing.

My team and I created a program for my peers that focused on leading through crisis. I sent out the agenda and a pre-read article from the *Harvard Business Review* titled "Are you managing or leading through the crisis?" My plan was to discuss the article for the first portion of the session. Then we could review our leadership behaviors and discuss how we could really help our employees with the crisis at hand. I started the session with a simple question.

"How are you doing?"

I received answers I didn't expect. Our Chief Operating Officer jumped in. He was concerned for his family, as well as our employees and business. Another executive said, with tears in his eyes, "I am scared." Then another, whose voice cracked as she spoke, expressed that she was stressed and anxious about what was going on.

I had planned to leave about fifteen minutes for this quick opening question. After about an hour and a half, our CEO Slacked me and said, "I know you have other topics you want to cover, but can we just let this continue?"

I replied, "Absolutely."

After about three and a half hours, everyone had let their feelings out. In my entire career, I have never seen an executive team show such raw, unfiltered emotion and pull together to support each other. After that session, we would check in with each other to see how we could offer further help and support.

The team then started to use that question with their respective teams by adding one simple word: "How are you doing... today?" This is a simple example of how easy it can be to check in with your employees, but you still need to be actively listening and processing their responses. Some leaders in the workplace may ask, "How is work going?" However, that is a very one-dimensional mindset. They are more than an employee; they are a multi-faceted human being. It's important to remember that.

Build Bridges, Not Walls

I am currently consulting to help a friend whose team started at 150 and then grew to 300. She kept reinforcing the need to establish a culture and wanted direction on how to meet the needs of her people in various time zones. Many leaders are still struggling with this because so many companies define culture only as what happens *at the office*, like back in the days when everyone commuted to the office five days a week.

I asked her, "Do you have a clear mission?"

Yes.

"Values?"

Yes.

A company's mission and values transcend physical walls. A big banking institution told their employees they had to be in the office three days a week for "innovation." However, innovation is not defined by operating in the same space. During COVID-19, Indeedians were in eleven thousand different places. During this timeframe, we innovated by producing our first Super Bowl ad, developing many new products, and effectively onboarding thousands of virtual employees.

The pandemic has shaken a lot of people because we like predictability and consistency. We like our groove, and anything outside of that makes us nervous. I recently gave a talk for leaders on the fear of the unknown.

Many leaders believe they will be able to go back to what is comfortable for them—the way they led pre-COVID-19. There is no going back. The pandemic crystallized it for me. You cannot go back to managing twelve people sitting around you as they once did. You cannot take them out to lunch or have water cooler conversations with them when they're no longer in proximity.

If you feel disconnected from your people or fragile in your understanding of what holds it all together, ask them and listen to their answers. Everyone is reassessing what is right for them. We need to allow each other time to process and find what works for us.

Listening for Mental Health

Everyone is grappling with how best to take care of themselves—and they should be! We're all built for reassessment and reinvention. Simultaneously, chaos, confusion, loss, and grief have been handed to us on a platter. As of late, what we've seen and experienced has been especially exacerbated by oddities and challenges. These were the news headlines in just 2020 alone: a green puppy, lions napping on the highway in South Africa, giant murder hornets, venomous caterpillars, and hungry monkeys taking over a city in Thailand. And of course, we had the pandemic as well! In 2022, we have had monkeypox, the return of polio, and several environmental disasters that jumped from the pages of a sci-fi book.

This is not about gloom and doom. This is about our reality. The status of our mental health is the foundation for coping with all that life throws at us. If you are not being an empathetic, expressive leader, you simply cannot be tending to this very foundation in yourself and others.

We've endured a lot, and we didn't have the luxury of plopping down on the highway and napping through it like the lions. The questions on everyone's mind should be: Do I need additional stressors? Can I cope with additional stress? Companies that succeed will see people as humans and understand their need for flexibility. They will also be open to thinking differently about where work gets done and how it is measured.

Where does the responsibility of a company start and stop when it comes to wellbeing? For so many of us, today's life model is work-life integration, and work-life balance is old hat. This means we're finding ways to integrate all the needs of our daily life. Maybe that means working in spurts rather than large blocks of uninterrupted time, maybe switching between answering work emails and doing yoga or other workouts. We can exercise more flexibility and fluidity (no pun intended), while maintaining strong boundaries between work and life. If you're not sure where you stand or sit on this spectrum, ask yourself if you are more of a balancer or integrator.

For so long, we leaned on the physical space we were in—the company-created space in which we functioned as workers—to enforce our workplace norms and culture. You could feel a vibe and energy practically bouncing off the walls when you were in the office. Everyone experienced this in some fashion. Now, flexibility in where and when you do your work is evolving as the new norm. There is no right or wrong answer. Everyone is trying to navigate new norms. It's about breaking the old paradigm of leading that we've learned to follow for so long. If you embrace change and think about leading differently, you will be a better leader, your team will be more engaged, and you will have better employees.

Some may feel forced to employ "servant leadership" because of what we've endured in the last three years. But we all must think differently about how we lead, how we work, and how we interact with each other. The business world can do better. It's time for this ripple effect to spread far and wide. Some people are already there, but not the vast majority.

A lot of the time when I was asked to provide advice or my opinion on an employee matter (performance improvement, behavioral issue, or termination), I would stop, take a breath, and ask, "How would you feel if this were happening to you, if your boss was doing this to you?" Asking probing questions like this will change perspective and inspire empathy.

People stop and contemplate this question. Often, they give excuses as to why they would "not be in situations like this."

My answer would be: "Well if you were, you wouldn't want to be put on a performance plan immediately. You would want another chance or more conversations with your leader that might clarify expectations and change the outcome."

Increased flexibility opens the door for us to show more vulnerability. It is okay to talk about why you're not doing your best that day or in that situation. You may be surprised how employees will feel a closer bond with their leader and that they will see them as a human too—not just a robotic leader who knows everything and never has an off day. Due to this very interaction, the bond may be stronger and the mission to do better will be more prevalent. Threading empathy into your interactions can fuel someone's desire to improve. I have been on both sides of the table in this situation many times.

We're all human beings. That one statement is true about everybody on the planet. It's so simple that we've all lost sight of it.

Personal issues will result in distracted employees. Individuals can compartmentalize, as it were, but consider what may be going on with that person that may not be visible to you—depression, anxiety, insomnia, heartbreak. It has happened to most of us. Keep this in mind as you make your next move, your next choice. You don't have to have an overwhelming emotional conversation at the moment. Rules, roles, and routines are still in place. You may have somewhere else to be or something else to tend to, but giving others that simple moment of understanding can make a huge impact on your mental health and that of your recipient.

These days, companies are getting taken to task because they may not have good mental health benefits—or any at all. Those of us who thought about the importance of offering mental health benefits were doing so long before the pandemic.

By June 2020, I had moved several hundred thousand dollars out of our "wellness incentive" fund and into "mental health benefits," so everyone could have access to virtual therapy. I still wanted to help everyone be healthy physically, but more immediately, I wanted to help them be healthy mentally. That summer, we were all dealing with a lot: a pandemic, financial uncertainty, the U.S. Presidential election, the reckoning around racism, plus anything else that people may have been experiencing personally.

Remember that an individual's story may include mental illness, even when the details or diagnosis is not yet clearly revealed. Consider the collective scope of mental health. According to facts and stats provided by the nonprofit Mental Health America:

- Nearly 1 in 5 American adults will have a diagnosable mental health condition in any given year.
- 46 percent of Americans will meet the criteria for a diagnosable mental health condition sometime in their life, and half of those people will develop conditions by the age of 14.
- 50 million U.S. adults have a mental illness.[19]

I will also underscore another statistic provided by MHA in the same quick facts sheet: 11 percent of adults with mental illness are uninsured. What treatment can they receive? If any, how are they paying for it? If they are not receiving treatment, how will the situation be exacerbated in the future? These are all daunting questions. The answers, the outcomes, have a real impact on the lives of these human beings and society as a whole.

We are finally normalizing conversations about mental health and mental illness in America. The fact that there is a stigma attached to something so fundamental to our existence as human beings is nonsensical. The BBC reports that

---

[19] Mental Health America, "Quick Facts and Statistics About Mental Health," Mental Health America, https://www.mhanational.org/mentalhealthfacts.

Some data shows stigma could be changing somewhat: in Mind Share Partners' 2021 study, 58 percent of study respondents were willing to hire or work with someone with a mental-health condition, which is 26 percent more than in 2019 (46 percent). Paula Allen, global leader and senior vice-president of research and total wellbeing at LifeWorks, believes one of the best things that came from the pandemic was that no-one could ignore their own vulnerability and that of the people around them. "We had a bit more empathy at the start of it," she says. "But that empathy was not fully sustained, and empathy alone is not enough to dislodge this kind of stigma."[20]

Work is a component of life. If all leaders could be better listeners and make a point to be present and empathetic, we could take a big step in stamping out this stigma for future generations. Let's start a practice of talking about the state of our health and really listening to one another. We all manage priorities other than work. Prioritizing flexibility and the overall health of individuals is crucial for companies in the war for talent. Job seekers will have to listen closely to glean just what flavor of flexibility a company is offering.

---

[20] Megan Carnegie, "Is workplace stigma around mental health struggles changing?" *BBC.com*, August 23, 2022, https://www.bbc.com/worklife/article/20220819-is-workplace-stigma-around-mental-health-struggles-changing.

AN EMPATHETIC, EXPRESSIVE LEADER'S PLAYBOOK
Listening as Sport
Greg Morley

Greg Morley is the Regional Human Resources Director for Asia-Oceania and the Global Head of Diversity, Equity, and Inclusion for Moët Hennessy, a division of LVMH (Louis Vuitton Moët Hennessy). Greg brings a personal and professional passion to developing talent and helping others achieve more than they believe they can. Before joining Moët Hennessy, he was Vice President of Human Resources Asia-Pacific for Hasbro, Inc. Prior to that, Greg was Vice President of Human Resources for the Shanghai Disney Resort in Shanghai, having also worked for Disney at locations in Hong Kong, Paris, and the U.S.

As of this writing, Greg is playing a leading role on the team working to bring the eleventh Gay Games to Hong Kong. The 2023 Gay Games will be a 12,000-participant event, celebrating sports, culture, and diversity. This will be the first time in its forty-year history that the games will be held in Asia.

Greg advocates that we treat listening as we would treat preparing to play a sport. It is not necessarily related to being competitive, other than being competitive with yourself to get the most out of you. Here are Greg's tips in his own words.

Preparation
Take time to prepare your thoughts and information in advance of listening to somebody during a session. Sometimes, this can be preparation for something like an interview. Other times, it may just be a discussion with a team member or even a friend. Preparation can take many forms. Looking someone up on social media (for example Google or LinkedIn) is a great way to understand a bit more about them and see what they may be interested in or curious about. You may also want to spend some time going back through notes you may have taken in

the past that can help you uplevel your active listening for the discussion to come.

Initiation
Setting the scene is critically important. Even in a casual session when you are trying your best to listen intently, you may start a conversation with a statement that lets the other person know that it is a safe space. I will often say to somebody that "the discussion we are having is between us," unless they ask me to share it or represent their thoughts and views to other people. These simple yet often overlooked steps encourage the other person in the discussion to be more open—and can make you a better listener in the process.

Active, intense listening
Active listening is a bit like meditation. Always try to clear your mind and bring yourself back to the person seated with you. It is human to have your mind wander as you're trying to be intently listening to somebody. Be aware of what the person is saying, how they're saying it, and where the conversation flows. Actively acknowledging them during the discussion is important to continue encouraging them to *share*.

Keep yourself engaged by using phrases like, "That's very interesting, could you tell me more about that?" Or simply just "Tell me more about that." These validating phrases will lead to further sharing. There will be a point in the conversation you may reach a natural pause. Before you wrap up ask, "What do you wish you had been able to share that you haven't already?" Finally, focus on trying to listen from the perspective of the other. This may be the most challenging skill and ultimately well worth practicing.

Clarifying
After having a good listening session with someone, it's a great opportunity to close by clarifying what you heard before

thanking your partner for their share. This is the perfect moment to recognize and encourage them so that, in the future, your partner will feel comfortable sharing and listening more. It takes two to make a splendid dance when it comes to sharing and listening.

Refreshing and relaxing for the next session

After you're done summarizing your conversation, take notes on what you heard. What went well, and what didn't go as well? If you had a conversation with someone you respect and believe could give you good feedback, ask them what they appreciated about your conversation, how they observed you listening to them, as well as what they believe you could do better next time. Sometimes, we are afraid to ask others for feedback. Almost every time you ask someone, they will take it as a recognition that you respect their opinion and your relationship with them. It's an honor to be asked for feedback, and we should all do it more frequently in recognition of those whose opinions we value.

I appreciate how Greg so clearly outlines these simple steps for being a great active listener. Being an active listener is a responsibility we must fully immerse ourselves in, blocking out all distractions, to be successful.

*"A smile is the light in your window that tells others
that there is a caring, sharing person inside."*

—DENIS WAITLEY,
International Speakers' Hall of Famer

CHAPTER 5

CARE

Everybody cares about this subject matter—the eight practices of empathetic, expressive leadership. Of course, it doesn't mean that care is always applied. This is not meant to be a provocative statement. I am simply declaring that we have lost sight of it. Is my declaration intriguing to you in some way? Have you ever felt like a robot or a machine in the workplace?

If you've watched *The Office*, you know that caring can go wrong! How it's depicted is quite comical. There is a line between being an employee and a friend. In our minds, we know where this line is. Sadly, Michael Scott did not. However, there are simple ways to demonstrate genuine care.

When I hear the word *love* in the workplace, my mind may gravitate to relationships, and relationships can be messy in the workplace. If we instead define love as *caring*, isn't that a trait we should all have? What has caring looked like where you have worked? When you are hired, you assume the company will care about you. Will it? Will your new leader care about you? What kind of care do you need? When we care about each other in a fundamental way, if we listen to each other's story, then we can determine more individualized support.

Expressing care may simply be taking someone to coffee and letting them bend your ear. The sweetest sound to just about anyone is their own name. People love to share and talk about themselves. Showing you care about someone who is struggling with mental health issues could be as simple as pointing them to some community or online resources. You do not need to recommend a therapist. Imagine how much it could mean to an employee to get a quick email message of thanks, encouragement, or congratulations! Spend ten minutes each morning crafting and sending a few of those. You must express your care and concern for people genuinely and not as an overblown reaction or a disingenuous display. (I've witnessed this many times, and these occurrences were not heartfelt.)

Empathy and Equity in Action

My husband and I have been together for twenty-seven years. I talk about him and our dogs in the workplace. There was one time, shortly after the addition of our newest family member (an eighteen-month-old puppy), when I made a comment about "our one-and-a-half-year-old." People thought I was referring to a human baby! A lot of us animal lovers may refer to our pets as babies or like people in other ways. I was congratulated on "the new baby" several times that week. You only need to glance in the dictionary to see that many words have more than one definition. Additionally, most people also have their own personal definitions that they use amongst their friends and family. Care enough to know if you're speaking the same language as the person you are interacting with.

In 1994, I was working for GE Capital in Roswell, Georgia, and I had been there a couple of months. We had a weekly business center leadership meeting. After one of these weekly meetings, a friend came to my office and asked, "Are you okay?" I said "Sure," but didn't have a clue why they were asking.

It turned out that someone had told a joke about a gay man, and I was the only out gay business leader there. Clearly, I hadn't been listening attentively in the meeting. I knew that my friend's concern for me was genuine.

A day went by, and two other leaders came to ask if I was okay. I was touched that so many of my colleagues expressed concern. They reflected, shared, saw, listened, cared. People showed me that they cared about me, the *real me*, enough that it sparked something within me. I had to show that same care for others like me. I wondered if the joke teller was a homophobe, and I felt like I had a responsibility to speak up. People were decidedly more empathetic and expressive in this situation than I was.

I found myself reporting an issue to HR for the first time in my career. On the way there, as I was replaying other interactions I'd had with this individual, I realized that this leader had made disturbing comments before. The HR business partner I reported the issue to seemed to have a standard response. "He's been here forever! Are you sure he said that? Are you sure he meant something by that? Maybe you didn't understand him."

I was concerned by her response, which seemed to show more caring for the leader than for me. It came across like she was grilling me for saying something offensive or embellished about her well-regarded leader. I told her, "No, I and others understood the joke exactly as it was meant to be understood, and you should do something about it!"

I reported the incident to the anonymous hotline at GE Corporate. The same HR business partner returned to me with, "You called the hotline?"

I said, "Yes, but I didn't want you to be the one following up on this."

Consequently, I escalated the issue to corporate HR. I said, "I don't need to be the poster child for this issue, but something needs to be done."

A representative from corporate HR interviewed both of us, after which the joke teller treated me differently. He stopped engaging me in conversation, and he stopped giving me projects. This was a situation in which someone in charge had an opportunity to empathize and do the right thing. Instead, it ended up being handled so poorly and things were made so miserable for me that I left the company. It was the first time I left a job without having another job. My mother, who had always insisted I have another job lined up—even if it was washing windows on a skyscraper in freezing rain—was probably rolling in her forever sleep over me leaving! But she was also a woman of integrity and authenticity, and I think she would have understood.

When I've talked about this experience, a few have asked, "That example of homophobia wouldn't happen today, right?" *But it does.* The homophobia, misogyny, xenophobia, ageism, and other forms of discrimination that exist in today's workplace are reflections of the world around us. What about people who come forward regarding sexual harassment only to be mocked, along with having their character and lives destroyed?

It is my job to know and care about every individual that I lead. If that HR business partner would have listened as a human being, maybe the situation would have ended differently. We could have gotten someplace together versus all the resulting animosity and my departure from the company. In my humble opinion, I would say that they lost an incredible employee.

I am a gay executive. We are all books with many chapters. Leadership goes hand in hand with being a role model within your company and your community. It is a vast responsibility—with infinite rewards if you are demonstrating empathy and expression.

Some of this caring is a basic instinct, that we automatically show to strangers or even the extended family members of our employees. I was two weeks into my new role as Chief HR Officer at a retail/catalog business owned by InterActiveCorp when I had the opportunity to act on this instinct. As I was walking through the distribution center on our campus in a suburb of Cincinnati, Ohio, I noticed several employees standing around another employee, who was laying on the ground. I went into emergency mode and ran over to ask what was going on. When I saw that the employee laying down was awake and responsive, I asked him what was wrong. He said that he felt lightheaded and passed out. He was still feeling very weak. I asked if anyone had called 9-1-1. The answer was, "No," so I called immediately.

We stayed with this employee, got him some water, and talked with him until the paramedics showed up. Once he was in the proper hands and on his way to being checked out, I went back to my office and called his emergency contact. It was his wife, who happened to be very upset. Our conversation was appropriately short, and she wrapped it up by telling me that she'd meet him at the hospital. The hospital was not far from our office. I couldn't get any info about them by calling the hospital, so after about ninety minutes, I decided to head over there for an update.

I asked about our employee in the ER, but I was told they could not give me any info, as I was not a family member. The receptionist pointed me to a woman sitting in the waiting room and said she was his wife. I went over to introduce myself and asked if I could sit down. She did not have any new information, other than they believed it may have to do with his diabetes. I changed the subject and asked her questions about herself, like how long they had lived in Cincinnati, if they had children, etc. We chatted on and off for about an hour, at which point the doctor came out and informed her that her husband was going to be okay. However, they'd need to keep a better check on his blood sugar.

Once I heard that he would be okay, I told her I was going to leave. I asked her to tell her husband to call if he needed anything, and I would not expect to see him until he was back to 100 percent. I returned to the office to finish out my day, then headed home exhausted. The next day I came in a little later than usual, and when I stopped by my assistant's office to check in, she pointed to a package on my desk. The employee's wife had dropped it off, a delicious-looking cake with a handwritten thank-you card. She expressed her thanks for me taking the time to come check on her husband. Most importantly, she was grateful for the idle conversation that kept her mind off what was going on with her husband.

R & R 2.0: Care to Give Rewards and Recognition

We all appreciate recognition and rewards (R & R) for the contributions we make. I've witnessed some leaders fall short in this area, while others have turned R & R into a huge extravaganza. Some leaders will demonstrate their care by creating a party-type culture, which reflects positively on them but doesn't recognize the individuals. However, what goes a long way for retention is one-on-one engagement. Giving your full attention to one individual, letting them know you care and that they are achieving great feats both in their development and for the sake of the company, is surely a best practice.

Remember that praise can be given at any time and often. Appreciation is lasting and can be conveyed to keep up morale and motivation. We have myriad devices for sending messages of recognition that can be crafted in seconds, and the positive effects of your words can last much longer than the time it took to express them.

Rewards are tangible displays that should be more periodic but just as meaningful. Today, we may have fewer spectacular trips and cocktail-filled fist-pumping summits to drum up big-team energy for meeting our goals in the next quarter. However, there are thousands of tangible gifts that can be delivered overnight. A caring reward can be transported quickly to the recipient you wish to recognize, no matter where they are located. You should never compromise or wait too long to show that you care. Express your appreciation while the job well-done is fresh in your mind.

My husband also has an HR background, in training and development specifically. In the early 2000s, he was working at The Disney Store headquarters in Glendale, California. He implemented a reward and recognition initiative in his department to allow colleagues to celebrate both professional and personal aspects of their lives. A weekly share-and-care session, if you will. Each Friday at 4:00 p.m., the entire HR department would gather in the training room for the "Fun Friday at Four" celebration.

Employees could share whatever they wished, both professional triumphs and personal plans or life updates. Everyone would then congratulate *the recruiters, who filled nine open positions* and *Trent, who completed all the graphics for the sales conference.* People could share their excitement about *Francine, who is taking her nephews to the zoo*, their support for *Tom, whose mom is having surgery*, and their happy wishes for *Jim, who has a birthday on Sunday.* The celebration could last anywhere from fifteen to forty-five minutes, and it always ended with a drawing for three gift cards to local restaurants, theaters, or stores. It was a wonderful, caring way to end the work week and begin the weekend. Not only did they get to bond as a company team, but also as full human beings.

Hiring, Firing, Inspiring

Several years ago, I was working at a large tech company as the Chief HR Officer. I had been there for two years as part of the leadership team. We were proud of our work and mission, and the team worked well together. Suddenly, without warning, our CEO was fired. He was loved and respected by everyone, but our parent company wanted a change. He was replaced by a CEO who had never been a CEO before.

In our first meeting, he said matter-of-factly, "I need to keep you happy because you're the guy that hires and fires people for me!" His tone was ominous, and he seemed to be oblivious to the fact that my role consisted of much more than just hiring and firing. After a few weeks, the new CEO decided to fire several members of the executive team, and he asked me to handle it. These people weren't just employees, they were great human beings.

Terminating someone is never fun, and, unless the employee did something egregious (like embezzling money or physically harming another employee), they are not a criminal. Yet, that is frequently how they are treated.

When he asked me to unceremoniously fire these executives, I decided that would not be my approach. In the days leading up to my meeting with each employee, I gave them clues by dropping subtle hints as to what the meeting was about. They picked up on my clues, although that did not make it any easier for me or them. Still, at least they were not taken by surprise. Plus, it may have inspired them to prepare for something better.

This wasn't intricate brain surgery. I just approached the situation with the perspective: *if this were me, how would I want to be treated?* I would want to be treated like a *human being*. What if we approached everything this way?

What if leaders and companies approached their roles from the perspective that we're all human beings first? Showing humanity in difficult times, like when you are tasked with letting someone go. Even if you do let them go, this approach will not only be appreciated, it will be remembered.

AN EMPATHETIC, EXPRESSIVE LEADER'S PLAYBOOK
Love Letters and Champagne

How can you show that you care? Make employee experiences better? Use their time wisely? Here are a few ideas of my own.

If someone on my team has a new baby, I turn to Omaha Steaks because of their prepared meals. It's difficult to find time to cook meals when you have a newborn! Still, everyone needs nourishment, so this is a great way to lighten their load and practice caring.

One day on a business trip, I was feeling particularly grateful for my team while walking and I stopped in a stationery shop. That night at the hotel, I hand-wrote cards for my team expressing my appreciation. I addressed each, stamped them, and dropped them off at the hotel concierge. Handwritten notes go a long way. Some people find handwritten notes incredibly meaningful, evening displaying them at home or on their desks at work. It's a simple but effective way to show you care. In the age of email and text, people lose sight of the fact that anyone can sit down and write something heartfelt.

When my former colleague, LaFawn Davis, was named in the "Top Queer 50" by *Fast Company*. I sent a bottle of champagne to her and her wife. They could enjoy it together while celebrating LaFawn's amazing achievement.

Showing that you care about your employees and colleagues is easy. Sometimes just remembering a birthday or work anniversary is meaningful to them. It goes a long way in showing the human side of leadership. It shows that leaders are human beings too.

"The business of business is relationships;
the business of life is human connection."

—ROBIN S. SHARMA,
Thought Leader on Stress Management and Spirituality

CHAPTER 6

CONNECT

Connected human beings and teams can overcome extreme challenges. Present me with any monumental effort, and I'll show you that there is typically a group of people to thank for getting it done. In general, human beings are designed to get along because we share a desire for love and belonging. This does not mean we don't all have unique characteristics, ambitions, and values—thankfully! Life would be bland, like yellow cake without icing, if we were all the same. We have extraordinary abilities in creativity and communication, which allow us to see world-changing projects through. All good leaders understand this, but it's easy to forget that accomplishments are rooted in our cognitive abilities, which we can enhance by putting our heads together.

According to Yuval Noah Harari's book, *Sapiens: A Brief History of Humankind*, at least six human species inhabited the

Earth one hundred thousand years ago. Think of all the brain power that wired the planet before us! Harari's description of the Cognitive Revolution, which brought new ways of thinking and communicating between seventy thousand and thirty thousand years ago, is profound. We only hear of the Industrial Revolution, but the Cognitive Revolution "witnessed the invention of boats, oil lamps, bows and arrows, and needles (essential for sewing warm clothing)." Harari continues, explaining that,

The earliest objects that can reliably be called art—such as the Stadel lion-man, an ivory figurine from the Stadel Cave in Germany—date from this era, as does the first clear evidence for religion, commerce, and social stratification. Most researchers believe that these unprecedented accomplishments were the product of a revolution in the Sapiens' cognitive abilities. They maintain that the people who drove the Neanderthals to extinction, settled Australia, and carved the Stadel lion-man were as intelligent, creative, and sensitive as we are today. If we were to come across the artists of the Stadel Cave, we could learn their language, and they could learn ours. We could explain everything we know—from Alice's Adventures in Wonderland to the paradoxes of quantum physics. They could teach us how their people view the world.[21]

This is a reminder that we, as a species, never needed automation, technology, or social media to think, feel, interact, and create.

---

[21] Yuval Noah Harari, *Sapiens: A Brief History of Humankind*, New York, New York: Harper, February 10, 2015.

Is This Place Really Safe?

Simple acts can foster new connections and deepen existing connections with other human beings. In most of the cities in which my husband and I have resided, we have lived in the suburbs. As a same-sex couple, we always have a little anxiety about moving into a new suburban neighborhood. In many, we have been the only same-sex couple, but by simply being ourselves and connecting with neighbors, we have made lifelong friendships.

In the most utopian world, we would see everyone for who they are. We would make new connections, deepen existing connections, and our stories would meld into one another. There would be a feeling of such resonance, there would be no room or time to focus on differences—let alone differences that divide us. If people would lead with curiosity rather than judgment, the undercurrent of tension and stress would subside.

Let's consider an example: starting a promising new position. You got the job, so you're feeling accepted, accomplished, and validated for your experience. When you arrive at your new workplace and join your new cohort, you may have the feeling of stepping into another country. You won't know what to expect for the first day, first week, or first month. While you're exhilarated and eager to explore and learn, you may also feel vulnerable and exposed.

If you've ever been to another country, you know the feeling. You are feeling overwhelmed! Luckily when you're traveling, you can dart back to your hotel to refresh or decompress. But in a new workplace, with your attention hyper-focused on your new role—and all of your coworkers' attention hyper-focused on you—a break may not come for a while. You may want to step away for some air, but you need to hang in there a while longer. When the others welcome you in a friendly and enthusiastic way, you'll begin to breathe easier. New connections are being made. Hopefully there will not be any pretense, negativity, or critical eyes on you in these early hours because everyone is in the same boat: you are all strangers getting to know one another, in the same predicament of meeting and greeting.

As the pace picks up, what you've learned will ignite the flames of responsibility and productivity. You may be extremely busy, completing tasks and attempting to keep up inside the larger nucleus of a company's operations. You're diligently fulfilling your role and earning your salary, but soon, you will have a clearer understanding of the company culture. Simply completing tasks by yourself at your desk will no longer be a satisfying position to find yourself in every day, a position at which you are likely to spend more time than anything else. You're seeking more engagement. Interacting with co-workers will immerse you in a culture that was well-established long before you arrived. You will discover your place and the influence you have in it. This is when you will get your initial sense of *psychological safety*, or the absence of it, and whether or not you *belong*.

What does psychological safety look like? Let's start with leadership scholar Amy Edmondson's definition:

> *When people on a team possess psychological safety, they feel able to ask for help, admit mistakes, raise concerns, suggest ideas, and challenge ways of working and the ideas of others on the team, including those in authority. Via this honesty and openness, risks are reduced, new ideas are generated, the team can execute those ideas and everyone feels included. Building psychological*

safety not only improves organizational outcomes, but it's the right thing to do.[22]

I also agree with *Forbes* contributor Timothy Clark, who writes, "Psychological safety is not a shield from accountability. It's not niceness, coddling, consensus decision making, unearned autonomy, political correctness, or rhetorical reassurance."[23]

For each person, this safety zone is going to look and feel differently because of their full range of lived experiences. Two baby boomers may feel psychologically safe in a different way than two Gen Zers. Generally, when baby boomers led the workforce, leaders had their work voice and work syntax. Then they went home and closed the door—to be immersed in their personal lives, to be themselves.

Separating your "work self" from your "real self" may stir up a sense of imposter syndrome, even if you're not calling it "imposter syndrome." The more psychologically safe we feel, the less we feel like we have to pretend to be someone or something we are not. The "imposter" is fed through feelings of incompetence despite our capabilities and achievements, and that self-doubt can come from the isolation of not belonging. Personality traits and mental health conditions can largely drive imposter syndrome. Some leaders are lucky enough to never experience this. But even without these compounding factors, who doesn't want to belong?

I was once in a new role in which the CEO started only a week after I did. We decided to host a town hall meeting to introduce

[22] Amy Edmondson, "Psychological safety and learning behavior in teams," *Administrative Science Quarterly*. 44. 250-282.
[23] Clark, Timothy, "What Psychological Safety Is Not," *Forbes*, June 21, 2021, https://www.forbes.com/sites/timothyclark/2021/06/21/what-psychological-safety-is-not.

ourselves and answer some employee questions. After we sent out the invite, I decided to speak off the cuff for my intro, so I did not write out any talking points.

When my CEO and I walked into the meeting, she kicked things off in a wonderful fashion with a joke. She proceeded to tell the company of her vast experience and that she was excited to be in this new role. I got up and talked about my experience at a sister company. Then I started talking about moving with my husband to this new city for the role.

There was a noticeable shift in the audience's energy, but I honestly wasn't sure what was going on. I was thinking to myself, *had I said something that upset people? Did I mispronounce a word?* I then stopped and simply asked the audience what happened. It felt like ten minutes of me standing up there waiting in silence, but it was probably more like ten seconds before an employee came to my rescue.

She politely asked, "Did you say your 'husband?'" I replied that I had and went on to explain further. Even though at the time gay marriage was not legal in this state or this country, we still referred to each other as "husbands." Suddenly, the audience burst into applause. It caught me completely off guard. As they quieted, I continued with my intro. Afterwards, we took questions for about twenty minutes.

As the meeting concluded, I saw that about twenty employees, including the woman who asked me the question, were waiting for me. This was before diversity, inclusion, and belonging became a must-do instead of a nice-to-have in the workplace. This group of employees had been waiting for someone like them. They told me that no leader at this company had ever stated that they were gay so casually and clearly. We sat in the cafeteria and talked for about an hour after the meeting.

Looking back on this interaction, this was probably my first real Employee Resource Group (ERG) meeting—and it was one that truly promoted belonging.

Deloitte's "2021 Human Capital Trends" report ranked *Belonging* as the top human capital issue that organizations face today.[24] Why does it matter? Belonging, besides establishing a culture of sharing and caring, impacts engagement and productivity in the workplace. A sense of belonging can lead to a 56 percent increase in job performance, a 50 percent reduction in turnover risk, a 167 percent increase in employer's net promoter score, two times more employee raises, eighteen times more employee promotions, and a 75 percent decrease in sick days.[25]

As human beings we are members of multiple cultures, which is a strength not a weakness. We can achieve more together than by ourselves. Culture should work for us and not undermine us. As leaders, we create and foster the culture for our team. We should be striving to create a culture of psychological safety and support—one where our employees can show up as the full human beings they are.

The advantages and bottom line of inspiring belonging are quite evident. When you don't feel belonging in the workplace, consider how the puzzle that makes up your being breaks into pieces. (Remember, *a workplace* includes screen-based environments and any prism involved in a job you work as an employee). Psych Safety UK explains the detrimental effects of nonbelonging clearly.

[24] Colleen Bordeaux, Betsy Grace, and Naina Sabherwal, "Elevating the Workforce Experience: The Belonging Relationship," *Deloitte*, November 2021. https://www2.deloitte.com/us/en/blog/human-capital-blog/2021/what-is-belonging-in-the-workplace.html.

[25] Colleen Bordeaux and Stephanie Lewis, "Designing the workforce experience with the human at the center," Deloitte, September 23, 2021. https://www2.deloitte.com/us/en/blog/human-capital-blog/2021/human-centered-workforce-experience.html.

An absence of shared characteristics, colleagues seeing you as different, together with feeling you are not adding value or making a positive contribution can also deepen the feeling of being an outsider.

When these factors combine at work, they can affect the very sense of who we are. It can undermine our self-esteem, our self-efficacy, and the clarity of our identity. This is because we so often attribute the cause of our sense of not belonging to ourselves—there must be something fundamentally wrong with us. This could be in terms of our personality or our competence, that resulted in our feeling excluded.[26]

Belonging Can Still Include (Healthy) Boundaries

When I talk about empathy, I am often asked about boundaries. For employers, and leaders specifically, where is the line between themselves and their people? Empathy should not be invasive. It is simply letting someone know that you understand and can relate to their situation or feelings. You may also share your perspective on how you have dealt with a particular issue. I don't think there is a universal answer. It depends on the situation.

For example, if someone asks for time off because of a "family matter," respect the way they are voicing this. If it were me receiving this request, I would respond with an empathetic statement, such as "I understand that family situations can be tough. I recently spent some time caring for and arranging medical appointments for my aunt when she was ill. Please continue to let me know what type of support you need from us."

---

[26] Psychological Safety, "What is Psychological Safety?", Psych Safety UK, https://psychsafety.co.uk/about-psychological-safety/.

This kind of sharing, that forges connections without crossing boundaries, can go a long way toward employee satisfaction, engagement, and retention.

If they are showing signs of distress, you may want to step in and inquire about further details or ask if you can do anything to assist. Remember the discussion on mental health. What is the best boundary a leader can draw here? The person may be suffering and might need help, and you may be among the few, or perhaps the only person who is hearing about their situation. It's very situational, so please use discernment. Ask questions to find out where lines are around every person, every situation. This is where understanding, sharing, and empathy apply. You must do the work to truly get to *know* the human being, before the crisis occurs. You must connect. Ask open-ended questions. Be curious, not judgmental.

Curiosity Saves... Lives, Leaders, Sanity, Blood Pressure

We possess IQ and EI, but when it comes to connecting with our people, my money also is on curiosity quotient or CQ. Think about when you go to a museum, nature center, or performance. If you're like me, you're dazzled and awestruck before much has even occurred! Just being in the physical space moves you and you anticipate that you will have a *spectacular* experience. What if you showed up to every interaction with your team like that? The *spectacular* could be found in a new detail you learn about someone. Perhaps it allows each of you to perform your respective roles better because of the enhanced engagement you will have gained.

In his book, *Da Vinci's Ghost: Genius, Obsession, and How Leonardo Created the World in His Own Image*, historian Toby Lester published one of Leonardo da Vinci's lists from 1490. A 2011 NPR

Opinion piece reviewed the book and reproduced the direct translation used in by Lester (plus a few amendments by NPR, bracketed for clarity).[27] Here are a few I found interesting:

- [Calculate] the measurement of Milan and suburbs
- [Find] a book that treats of Milan and its churches, which is to be had at the stationer's on the way to Cordusio
- [Discover] the measurement of the Corte Vecchio [courtyard of the duke's palace]
- Get the master of arithmetic to show you how to square a triangle
- Ask Maestro Antonio how mortars are positioned on bastions by day or night
- Ask Bendetto Portinari [a Florentine merchant] by what means they go on ice at Flanders
- [Ask about] the measurement of the sun, promised me by Maestro Giovanni Francese
- [Examine] the crossbow of Maestro Gianetto
- Draw Milan
- Find a master of hydraulics and get him to tell you how to repair a lock, canal, and mill, in the Lombard manner.

"It is useful," Leonardo wrote, "to constantly observe, note, and consider." Indeed! Admittedly, my to-do list may be mundane—with tasks such as checking on my many bird feeders, playing with the dogs, and once again, discussing what we should have for dinner with my husband. Imagine the surge of curiosity that fueled a list like da Vinci's. Each task screams of curiosity and

---

[27] Krulwich, Robert, "Leonardo's To-Do List," NPR.org, November 18, 2011, https://www.npr.org/sections/krulwich/2011/11/18/142467882/leonardos-to-do-list.

imagination—expressing a desire for better understanding, better collaboration, and better results.

Psychologists, anthropologists, economists, historians, and philosophers have all studied curiosity to better understand mental health, physical health, buying trends, societal progress, and the direct correlation to connection. A curious human creates a feeling of connection.

Jill Suttie wrote about "why curious people have better relationships" for Berkeley's Greater Good Science Center magazine, aptly titled *Greater Good*.

Studies have found that people who are curious are often viewed in social encounters as more interesting and engaging, and they are more apt to reach out to a wider variety of people. In addition, being curious seems to protect people from negative social experiences, like rejection, which could lead to better connection with others over time.[28]

In contrast, some of us have been programmed by experiences and outside influences to pre-judge people based on their physical appearance, what they are wearing, what they sound like, or their vocabulary. It's what makes instilling diversity, inclusion, and belonging more challenging in the twenty-first century. It makes it more difficult for people to get along, collaborate and contribute.

When you meet someone who is different from you or who states an opinion that is different from yours, try asking

---

[28] Jill Suttie, "Why Curious People Have Better Relationships," *Greater Good Magazine*, May 31, 2017, https://greatergood.berkeley.edu/article/item/why_curious_people_have_better_relationships.

open-ended questions. Instead of reacting immediately or jumping to judgment, seek to understand why.

- "Why is that your opinion?"
- "What is the tradition?"
- "How did you reach that conclusion?"
- "What is the story behind this?"

The goal in gathering this information is not to change your opinion—or theirs. However, over time you will learn to *respect* that their opinion is different from yours, and appreciate that they shared it with you. They have valid reasons why they believe something. Simply allow them to share.

How do you connect to someone with whom, on the surface, you have very little in common? Curiosity. How do you make deeper connections? Curiosity. We will always find commonality when we go beyond the physical; there will always be something new to learn. Elicit that new information and harness it for enhanced engagement. Leading with curiosity creates a more collaborative, electric learning environment. Demonstrate your curiosity by simply asking questions or framing the conversation with phrases like, "Let's look at this a different way," or "What comes to mind when you think of..."

In her piece for *Greater Good Magazine*, Suttie describes how curiosity simultaneously improves relationships with oneself and others in multiple ways. For example: curious people cope better with rejection, are less aggressive, and tend to enjoy socializing more. Think of how powerful the switch from judgment to curiosity can be! The treasures of curiosity can be accessed anytime, as we can choose to activate them simply by taking a short pause.

A Case of Extreme Empathy

Have you heard of the Empathy Museum? This is not just another example from the utopia that I hope empathetic, expressive leadership will create. It really does exist! Founded by philosopher Roman Krznaric in 2015, the museum offers:

> a series of participatory art projects dedicated to helping us look at the world through other people's eyes. With a focus on storytelling and dialogue, [the] traveling museum explores how empathy can not only transform our personal relationships, but also help us tackle global challenges such as prejudice, conflict, and inequality.[29]

Krznaric has also coined the term, "experiential empathy." In his mesmerizing piece, "Empathy Heroes: 5 People Who Changed the World by Taking Compassion to the Extreme," Krznaric introduces readers to the U.S. product designer Patricia Moore, who's specialized in using empathy to address cross-generational biases.

> Her best-known experiment was in the late 1970s when, aged 26, she dressed up as an 85-year-old woman to discover what life was like as an elder. She put on makeup that made her look aged, wore fogged-up glasses so she couldn't see properly, wrapped her limbs and hands with splints and bandages to simulate arthritis, and wore uneven shoes so she hobbled.
>
> For three years she visited North American cities in this guise, trying to walk up and down subway stairs, open department store doors, and use can openers with her bound hands.

[29] "What Is Empathy Museum?" Empathy Museum, https://www.empathymuseum.com/.

The result? Moore took product design in a completely new direction. Based on her experiences, she invented new products for use by elders, such as those thick rubber-handled potato peelers and other utensils now found in almost every kitchen, which can easily be used by people with arthritic hands. She went on to become an influential campaigner for the rights of senior citizens, helping to get the Americans With Disabilities Act enacted as law.[30]

What would happen to us if we walked in someone else's shoes for a day, at least once, to connect to their experiences? It doesn't have to be three years! However, I am thoroughly inspired by Patricia Moore's heightened empathy, dedication, and bravery. Her product designs and campaigns for policy changes were very literally life-changing. I would imagine that she feels extremely connected to the population she transformed herself to be a part of. Now that she is in her 70s, I wonder if she benefits from some of her own discoveries.

I'm not sure I ever think of leadership without empathy. Moore seems to have deep practice in both types of empathy identified by contemporary researchers and defined as the following in *Greater Good Magazine*:

"Affective empathy" refers to the sensations and feelings we get in response to others' emotions; this can include mirroring what that person is feeling or just feeling stressed when we detect

---

[30] Roman Krznaric, "Empathy Heroes: 5 People Who Changed the World By Taking Compassion to the Extreme," *yes!* November 7, 2014, https://www.yesmagazine.org/health-happiness/2014/11/07/empathy-heroes-st-francis-john-howard-griffin-patricia-moore.

another's fear or anxiety. "Cognitive empathy," sometimes called "perspective taking," refers to our ability to identify and understand other people's emotions.[31]

"Continue to Bring You"

My best friend, Pam, and I share a lot of the same values, and it is within those values that she influenced my leadership style. She is a retired attorney. We met one day at the neighborhood mailboxes in our shared cul-de-sac. She ended up representing me in a matter involving my mom's death, and later became my greatest mentor and friend. Pam practiced law in South Florida for over twenty years. She represented the government at varying levels throughout her career, followed by years of working in employment discrimination law, including representing a couple of labor unions. Later, she mostly handled unemployment matters. She represented both management and employees, and saw a lot in the process.

Pam understands that my goal is for leadership to appreciate and utilize HR for success. Instead of seeing HR as a burden, they could choose to see it strictly as a benefit. She heard my anxiety when it was at its worst, while I was managing the expansion of my role at the height of the pandemic. Money did not drive me. My concern for my employees did.

The desire (and effort) to maintain one's image often counters the behaviors that allow for a healthy workforce, and this is not unique to my employer at the time. Pam reminded me that I was not a public relations professional, responsible

[31] "Empathy Definition: What Is Empathy." *Greater Good Magazine*. https://greatergood.berkeley.edu/topic/empathy/definition.

for keeping up the company's image to so many employees. I needed to master being realistic. I could stay connected to employees and colleagues through all of the uncertainty. On the tough days, that would get me through.

One aspect of an HR leader's role is determining how laws should apply. In all that law juggling, where does inclusion fit? "In all your interactions, continue to bring you," Pam reminded me. My connection with Pam and her ability to center me amid turmoil was part of what drove me to craft the message about my OCD, the message that elicited about four hundred responses. Sharing our own stories connects all of us in some way.

Pause for a moment. What are you going through today that you could share? Who might you help by creating this bid for connection? Who seems isolated lately? Who didn't perform well on a task that they usually nail? Do you know why? Reflect, share, see, listen, care, and *connect to see if you can find the answers.*

These connections will go on to inform and impact you throughout your career. As connected as we are, I still learn more about Pam all the time. Just recently I learned that she doesn't eat cheese! You can continue to make different connection points and learn about those who are already part of your network. The more you learn, the richer those connections will be. And as you connect relationships from multiple areas of your life, they will continue to enrich one another.

AN EMPATHETIC, EXPRESSIVE LEADER'S PLAYBOOK
Candy Still Delights

I credit this concept to American Express: The candy dish on the desk. In the early 90s, I knew a supervisor in customer service at American Express who kept a jar full of candy on his desk. I said, "Wow, you must love chocolate."

He said, "I hate chocolate." *Huh?* Curiosity struck. "I don't need to love it. People don't want to generally come back here and have a conversation because they think something bad is going to happen to them. It's a way to lure your team over to mill about, chat," he explained.

Shortly after this conversation, I placed a bowl of candy on my desk, and it worked. Everyone on the tenth floor in the New York City Indeed office knew I had candy. On a bad day, I would consume three mini-Snickers myself and be done with it. Throughout the day, however, the candy level in the bowl would decrease because people were stopping by and connecting with me. As it turned out, the conversations became more casual and less focused on work, which was a fantastic way to learn, relate, and get to know the people around me.

My husband has also used this same candy tactic to his great advantage at work. What a simple way of connecting to so many human beings! There are lots of variations in ways to connect. Don't forget about quick virtual coffee chats and guest speakers that set the motivational or inspirational tone for the day.

"Our prime purpose in this life is to help others.
And if you can't help them, at least don't hurt them."

—HIS HOLINESS THE 14TH DALAI LAMA

HELP. What a gargantuan word lately. I need help. How can I help? Is there help for this problem? How do we help those in greater need? Help wanted.

As discussed, early on in COVID-19, Indeed decided to close all offices, worldwide. We had eleven ERGs, including a new one for parents and caregivers. I suggested meeting with the chair of this ERG because I wanted to know how we could better serve the parents. Schools were closing, and children were learning virtually. The ERG chair listed five action items, although not all five were practical or within our power and resources. However, two of them were completely doable. We could ensure managers were supportive of parents' needs during this time—allowing for alternate work schedules and being open to re-prioritizing projects. We could also provide general support for parents and work with vendors to provide virtual learning opportunities for children not yet in school.

Though optimistic, I don't live with a utopian worldview that everything is automatically *the best*. What do you think about your own development or training? Realistically, it involves you getting better, not becoming the best in an instant. Incrementally, you take steps and get better over time. Things are always changing. Someone needs help—or you need help. We must have the courage to ask for it.

What Hinders Help

Distrust

For some, asking for help is a *big* ask. Admitting you need help requires *trust*. This is true from the bottom to the top of an organization. Whether it is on the board, within the customer base, or in the community—wherever humans congregate trust is important., It doesn't matter if the people touch the product or what kind of service is being rendered or consumed. Trust reigns supreme, and it reveals itself in times of crisis and stability.

I like this overarching definition of trust by Dennis Jaffe writing for *Forbes*.

The glue of society is called trust. Its presence cements relationships by allowing people to live and work together, feel safe, and belong to a group. Trust in a leader allows organizations and communities to flourish, while the absence of trust can cause fragmentation, conflict and even war.[32]

---

[32] Dennis Jaffe, "The Essential Importance of Trust: How to Build It or Restore It," *Forbes*, December 5, 2018, https://www.forbes.com/sites/dennisjaffe/2018/12/05/the-essential-importance-of-trust-how-to-build-it-or-restore-it/.

Think of the magnitude of the distrust of the large entities that govern our lives that has spread recently, darkening our days and our perceptions of these institutions. It spanned across public health, medicine, law enforcement, and government. We have seen the magnitude of damage that can be done.

What about the institutions of business and family? When distrust seeps into these environments, it can be devastating. The pandemic was a real threat to security and mental health, both for ourselves and our families. Distrust in the workplace is like a virus, infecting and harming culture. It is not conducive to team members and leaders asking for help when they may need it the most. The bonds created through trust impact mentoring and training. It is important on every level for each of us in our daily lives.

Global communications firm Edelman has a longstanding story about trust, which they have studied trust for more than twenty years. They

> *believe that it is the ultimate currency in the relationship that all institutions—business, governments, NGOs, and media—build with their stakeholders. Trust defines an organization's license to operate, lead and succeed. Trust is the foundation that allows an organization to take responsible risk, and, if it makes mistakes, to rebound from them. For a business, especially, lasting trust is the strongest insurance against competitive disruption, the antidote to consumer indifference, and the best path to continued growth. Without trust, credibility is lost, and reputation can be threatened.*[33]

---

[33] Edelman, "Why We Study Trust," Edelman.com, https://www.edelman.com/trust.

In 2020, Edelman's annual Trust Barometer tracked 40 global companies over the course of a year (marked by a global pandemic no less). They "learned that ethical drivers such as *integrity, dependability,* and *purpose* drove 76 percent of the trust capital of business, while *competence* accounted for only 24 percent."[34]

Trust advances society, businesses, and teams. It can be earned and lost at any time. In fact, trust is dependent on time because it "is built slowly, through repeated interactions." That is according to organizational behavior researchers Alisa Yu, Julian Zlatev, and Justin Berg in their piece, "What's the Best Way to Build Trust at Work?" in *Harvard Business Review*.[35] Their advice is informed by six studies in which they "looked at the role emotional acknowledgment, or the act of verbally recognizing someone else's feelings." They explain that emotional acknowledgment

> *plays an important role in a wide variety of high-stakes and low-stakes situations—from employee socializing in a break room to hospital workers navigating intensive care units. Drawing on the* costly signaling theory, *which states that small gestures can make a big impact, they aimed to discover how emotional acknowledgment influences* interpersonal trust.

It's worth noting that *interpersonal trust* is defined as the perception you have that other people will not do anything that will harm your interest; the individual is given the willingness

---

[34] https://www.edelman.com/trust/2020-trust-barometer.
[35] Alisa Yu, Julian Zlatev, and Justin Berg. "What's the Best Way to Build Trust at Work?" *Harvard Business Review.* June 18, 2021. https://hbr.org/2021/06/whats-the-best-way-to-build-trust-at-work.

to accept vulnerability or risk based on expectations regarding another person's behavior.

Confirmation bias

Confirmation bias is a phenomenon wherein decision-makers have been shown to actively seek out and assign more weight to evidence that confirms their hypothesis. They also ignore or under weigh evidence that could disconfirm their hypothesis.

Studies have shown that once someone has formed an initial judgment or opinion about something, there is a strong tendency to reaffirm that assessment. This is done by intentionally seeking out evidence that will confirm or reinforce that point of view, and people will deny or intentionally avoid considering any evidence to the contrary.

Using meaningful examples from their marriage to underscore the "perils of confirmation bias," social workers Linda Bloom and Charlie Bloom wrote in *Psychology Today* that "confirmation bias suggests a lack of perceiving circumstances objectively."[36] You pick out those bits of data that make you feel good because they confirm your preconceived beliefs. When this happens, you become unable to reassess your perspective, and your assumptions become your hardcore truths. For obvious reasons, permitting confirmation bias to be your fixed mindset can be very limiting to your personal development and dangerous to relationships. The danger is that when you don't collect or even remain open to processing new information that may help you to update assumptions, your conclusions may no longer be

---

[36] Linda and Charlie Bloom, "Beware of the Perils of Confirmation Bias," *Psychology Today*, July 9, 2018, https://www.psychologytoday.com/us/blog/stronger-the-broken-places/201807/beware-the-perils-confirmation-bias.

accurate or valid. Confirmation bias often leads to attachments that swell into prejudices against situations and people.

Warning against feeding a "closed loop of defensiveness and antagonism," which can negatively characterize any relationship, the Blooms state the following.

Being a permanent prisoner of confirmation bias involves the greatest loss of all: the loss of the freedom to make conscious, responsible choices for our own life based upon trustworthy, informed, and accurate information, rather than conditioned beliefs that may no longer be valid or relevant to our current reality.

In working with so many human beings, I have vividly seen all that the Blooms talk about and the distinctions they make. Product teams minimizing constructive feedback from user groups and focusing on the positive feedback. HR teams downplaying critical feedback about a leader because they have been there for a long period of time. Leaders, who truly should not be leading because of their bad behavior, allowed to stay in their roles due to senior management's belief that they are too smart to lose. I'm sure I have also been the culprit of perpetuating these assumptions, but I continually strive to be a better human being, a better leader, whose main objective is to help.

In a candid blog on his company's website, Nick Mehta distinguishes between human-inspired CEOs and war-time CEOs. Both breeds have been handily referenced over the past few years. At the heart of his message is humanity in business and creating psychological safety for an entire workforce, not simply people with similarities. He writes,

Human-first CEOs are reconsidering the makeup of their workforce and assessing if their representation is in line with the overall demographic mix of the population. While companies have made strides in gender representation in the last few years, much more is left to be done. And technology companies have shockingly little to report in terms of progress around Black and Latinx employees. Human-first CEOs realize that this situation must change.[37]

If we're not helping our whole team by considering their lived experiences, we're not helping. We may be helping one individual or group while simultaneously harming another by making them feel less important and isolated. Mehta reports a happier, more helpful outcome that changing times sparked in his company. In the same post, he writes,

My hopes and beliefs were validated when my CEO group gathered again recently. The same leaders who were reluctant to discuss social issues in 2019 were reassembled the week after George Floyd's death and the conversations were 100 percent about justice and equality. Whether the dialog was driven by genuine compassion or a desire to adapt to the new mainstream, nonetheless the discussion finally happened.

Asking for Help is Negotiation Practice on Steroids

In their book, *Getting to Yes: Negotiating Agreement Without Giving In* (now in its third edition), Roger Fisher, William Ury, and

---

[37] Mehta, Nick, "The World Needs Human-first CEOs, Not War-time CEOs," *Gainsight*, https://www.gainsight.com/blog/the-world-needs-human-first-ceos-not-war-time-ceos/.

Bruce Patton[38] emphasize *mutual-gains negotiation* or *integrative negotiation.* Bargainers seek negotiation strategies that can help both sides acquire gains. By listening to each other, treating each other fairly, and exploring options to increase value, negotiators can find ways of "getting to yes" without relying on aggressive tactics and bitter concessions.

Co-author William Ury is one of the world's leading negotiation specialists and co-founder of a slew of groundbreaking projects centered on building consensus. Ury's past clients include dozens of Fortune 500 companies, and even the White House, where a "no" or "yes" could result in dire consequences for the country or the world.

The authors describe six negotiation principles in *Getting to Yes* that can apply to every ask that could come out of a human being's mouth:

1. *Separate the people from the problem.* Don't forget that your counterparts have feelings, opinions, and reasons that contribute to what they do and say. Avoid the tendency to blame.

2. *Focus on interests, not positions.* By understanding what interests the other party has, you may see commonalities to capitalize on.

3. *Learn to manage emotions.* Exercise freedom of expression on both sides. Free expression automatically constructs a safety zone and trust.

4. *Express appreciation.* Words and actions of appreciation build an alliance, even if only for one specific ask. Impasses are

---

[38] Roger Fisher, William Ury, and Bruce Patton, *Getting to Yes,* New York, New York: Penguin Random House, 2011.

much easier to break when the other person feels appreciated for their contributions.

5. *Put a positive spin on your message.* It's very simple: Communicating in a positive way is a much more effective means of getting a yes than criticizing or blaming. Instead of speaking on behalf of a group, which may feel like intimidating or restrictive groupthink, speak for yourself only.

6. *Escape the cycle of action and reaction.* The authors introduce a negotiation skill they call *negotiation jujitsu*, or avoiding escalation by refusing to react. Channel your resistance into more productive negotiation strategies, such as, "Exploring interests, inventing options for mutual gain, and searching for independent standards."

Why talk about negotiation? There is no negotiation without asking a lot of questions or without emotional intelligence. Businesses do not exist without negotiation. With practice, you get used to asking for and receiving assistance. Help does not have to come in the form of a hard transaction (I need food; feed me!)—the request can be framed inside of a conversation, exploring solutions together. After a discussion, the best solution might be to delegate some tasks. Delegation is always an acceptable, appreciated, and expected form of help. Companies do not function properly without it.

When I was leading teams, I would hire people that possessed skills and expertise that I did not necessarily have. A good example of this is keeping our budget updated and current. In my last position, I admitted that I was not great at this and looked for a chief of staff who possessed this skill.

I hired one who was masterful at budgeting and so much more. What a find!

Senior leaders run into walls with tasks that they are not skilled in or that they simply abhor doing. However, they rarely ever ask for help. Why is asking for help in the workplace considered bad? Imagine not admitting a shortcoming, then trying to get a task or project completed while your stress overtakes you and feelings of inadequacy make you question and punish yourself. In this case, you would be an imposter! Your work will suffer. You may become physically ill. It may result in you being unable to work at all. Your teams suffer. How could this be a noble thing? Refraining from expressing a need is not a strength. It smothers possibilities and opportunities.

If you want to get philosophical, think about this undue stress. The other part of this equation is that you must be in a space of psychological safety that allows you to ask for help. When a leader shows vulnerability and empathy, this creates an environment of speaking up, sharing, and exchanging feedback. Asking for help shows strength, openness, and willingness to accept new ideas and perspectives. If people see you struggling but not admitting it, how does that foster transparency in conversations? The sooner you can be transparent about what you do not know, the quicker your people can rally and find the knowledge or solution needed. Your ask for help is also a call for collaboration, which instantly engages and empowers. These are ingredients that need to be included in the recipe of empathetic, expressive leadership. The sheer act of expressing that you need help makes you relatable and makes others feel valued.

AN EMPATHETIC, EXPRESSIVE LEADER'S PLAYBOOK
Rescue Missions
Irene Brank

You never know what kind of help someone will need. Sometimes it's drastic, what Irene Brank, who leads a Learning and Performance Team, calls "rescue missions." She serves as her company's Pride ERG Vice Chair, Transgender Liaison & Gender Transition Partner. Long before stepping into the spotlight that this title brought to her inside her organization (an "insurance" company at that—talk about nuances of the eight practices), Irene embarked on a rescue mission a her own: to take care of her daughter. Irene supported her daughter, Samantha, through her coming out as a transgender person as a teenager and through her journey of accessing gender-affirming care and surgeries.

Known as @_samanthalux online, Samantha is a YouTube content creator who has amassed over six hundred thousand subscribers and sixty million channel views in the last few years.[39] The transition was tough for the whole family, but now, Irene and Samantha share their experience globally. Together they use their platform to promote social change, specifically aiming to reduce prejudice regarding the transgender community. Irene has helped numerous transgender people, in her company and others, and their families by sharing invaluable resources, ranging from how to get legal advice and maneuver medical care to job protection and financial challenges.

When I spoke with Irene, her performance of the eight practices of empathetic and expressive leadership was evident, both at

---

[39] First Event 2023, "Samantha Lux," First Event 2023, https://firstevent.org/samantha-lux/.

home and work. "It started with my kid, who is a human being," she said. "In 2016, I was named as a transgender liaison for the Pride Business Resource Group at my company. Many people knew about Samantha at that point.

"Again, I would have never guessed that I would be entrenched in LGBTQ+ rights. But that's the beauty of life—sheer surprise. Every time that I wanted to back down or felt tired, I thought of Samantha's courage. Word spread that I was a parental expert in the 'T', and I started getting calls to speak publicly. Usually, I would be asked to tell the story about my daughter. During one such event, a man asked, 'How do I get to people? How do I drive change?' I said, 'Tell stories. That is how you get to people.' You start with their hearts, and their minds come along.

"It is impossible to not relate in some way. Moms are moms everywhere in the world and keep the world's population going. I use my past experience and what I continue to learn, in order to help my company and others continue to grow their knowledge around transgender and non-binary people. At an insurance company, there are not only the employee aspects but the insurance aspects. What if an employee or a client wants to change their gender in our systems? How should we approach these and other situations? How do we ensure we are treating people with respect, inclusion, and equity? The answer is with knowledge, empathy, and understanding. The easiest example is exploring why pronouns matter. Pronouns may seem like the simplest part of the sentence for most of us, but for a transgender person they are [very] important. We can all 'do better'."

Irene is taking "helping" to another level—she is changing lives! Using her dual role as a mother and business leader to inform her knowledge and empathetic nature sets an example for so many.

As she says, who doesn't relate to being a mom? Or if you're not a parent, what about the relationship you have with your best friend or partner? How can the details of their life experiences that you've been directly influenced or impacted by inform your legacy as a leader? Chances are someone in your company needs to hear from you. You don't have to stand on the big stages to say what matters, according to Tricia Brouk, noted public speaking coach and author of The Influential Voice.

In her book, Brouk writes: "I have learned time and time again that saying what matters does create change. And sometimes, you don't necessarily have time to prep. A powerful example is when Fred Guttenberg, whose fourteen-year-old daughter, Jaime, was killed by a single bullet in the back when she was running for her life at Stoneman Douglas High School on Valentine's Day, 2018.

"He had this to say for The Influential Voice: 'The moment that defined everything I do wasn't my daughter being murdered—it was the next day when I stood up at a vigil in front of approximately one thousand people. I went to the vigil with my sister and friends. My wife and son didn't go, but I felt that I needed to be around people. When I got there, Christine Hunschofsky, the mayor of Parkland, Florida, asked me to speak. I didn't prepare for it, but I went up there and spoke. It lit me on fire.'" According to Brouk, that night became a defining time that set him on the path of fighting gun reform legislation.[40]

---

[40] Tricia Brouk, The Influential Voice, Franklin, Tennessee: Post Hill Press, April 27, 2021.

*"The desire for safety stands against
every great and noble enterprise."*

—TACITUS,
Ancient Roman Historian

CHAPTER 8

PROTECT

Sometimes being a human being is simple when we have our values intact. *Fair, good, honest,* and *better* are my fundamentals. I have always said that there are two lines I will not cross in my job as head of HR—nothing illegal or unethical. There is always an "HR way" to do everything, and it's not necessarily the most effective or profitable way for the business. I was asked once by a CEO to do something that felt very squarely in the gray area of the ethics world. I told him I would not do it, partly to protect myself. However, I was also protecting him and the organization in its entirety by objecting to his demand. My opposition had him reconsidering his request. I believe I even used the word "protect," which is a strong word in that setting. It is also a strong action that encapsulates the other seven practices of empathetic and expressive leadership. Otherwise, the house of cards falls.

In business, we hear a lot of talk about protecting brands, entities, and even their leaders. I rarely hear about protecting the human beings that are so dedicated to their teams and companies. Thankfully, you can protect them through the culture you establish by including psychological safety, as well as other practices and policies that promote their well-being.

HR in View

Though HR-focused influencers may not be as highly followed as other types, I do recommend Jessica Miller-Merrell (@jmillermerrell across the Internet). According to her website, she is a workplace change agent, author, and consultant who focuses on human resources and talent acquisition. Recognized by *Forbes* as a "Top 50" social media influencer, she's the founder of Workology, a workplace HR resource, and host of the "Workology Podcast."[41] The greatest portion of her audience is at the executive level, to whom she emphasizes a contemporary approach to HR practices. In addition, she freely shares HR organizational charts, department structures, and job descriptions in great detail. To my knowledge, I've not seen work like hers previously in the public sphere.

In my own experience as an HR executive, I've been asked questions like:

- "What do you people do in HR?"
- "If you're the people department, why can't you fight to increase my salary, my benefits?"
- "Isn't HR just the fixer to all the executive team's screwups?"

---

[41] Jessica Miller-Merrell, "About," *Workology.com*, https://workology.com/about/work-with-workology/.

Questions like this can be hurtful and harmful, diminishing the profession and the impact it has on an entire workforce. That's not why the HR department exists. There are aspects of these roles where you can reinforce the *human* in human resources.

But where exactly are those opportunities to prioritize the *human* in human resources? Consider Miller-Merrell's summary of an HR organization and team structure, which is aligned with my twenty-plus years of experience:

The HR organization and HR departments are evolving from administrative departments that lead the transactional HR activities of record-keeping, payroll, and employee benefits administration into teams led by C-level executives and directors who report to C-suite. According to a report produced by the Cranfield Network on International Human Resource Management in collaboration with SHRM called Human Resources Management Policies and Practices in the United States, *70 percent of responding organizations said HR has a place on the board of directors, and 66 percent reported having a written HR management strategy. Responses also indicated that HR is taking sole responsibility for major policy decisions. This evolution has seen the creation of new positions like Chief Diversity Officer (CDO), Chief Human Resources Officer (CHRO), and changes in who the Vice President of HR or CHRO reports to.*[42]

With different tiers, each filling different functions to proactively display and advocate for empathetic, expressive

[42] Jessica Miller-Merrell, "HR Organizational Chart and Department Structures," *Workology.com*, January 10, 2022, https://workology.com/your-guide-to-the-hr-organizational-chart-and-department-structuresstructure-functions/.

leadership, HR employees set the tone and play a fundamental role, with *protection* as the primary goal of these eight practices. We've been taught certain ways of doing things. For example, the term "investigation" gets thrown around a lot, and it puts people on the defensive. It sounds like a legal term. HR professionals can still perform reviews or (gritting teeth) *investigations* without using the off-putting terms and language associated with them. The HR business partner has the role of interfacing with employees.

Here is an example of what I think a "human being first" approach to an investigation might look like:

John has been a mediocre performer this week. He is not speaking up in meetings. He was ill-prepared for the client presentation. What else is going on with John? The company can afford to isolate this one week and then check in with John to let him know they are aware of "something"—giving him the benefit of the doubt. However, when that one week goes unchecked and turns into a few months, then you have a severe situation. John is getting paid to do a job, but there could be external factors that are causing his performance and light to be dimmer.

If you discover that these factors are not business-related, you still should take them into account. There are things you can do to help, using empathy and sympathy.

Realizing that workers have stressors going on outside the work arena kickstarts an inclination towards understanding. There are companies out there paying people to *not* check their email during vacations. Imagine that! Perhaps they do so to protect the company, because they know that productivity dwindles after fifty or so hours on the clock, and that burnout and overload can lead to zapped brainpower (creativity, communication skills, critical thinking, high analysis).

I'm not suggesting leaders become friends with all of the employees. Familiarity is a personal choice. At the same time, global analytics and advice firm Gallup does illustrate through recent data that having friends at work is key to employee engagement and job success. An article from August 2022, titled "The Increasing Importance of a Best Friend at Work," linked workplace friendships to improved business outcomes, including profitability, safety, inventory control, and retention. Gallup has studied employment engagement for eighty years with the mission of building exceptional workplaces. They assert that, employees who have a best friend at work are significantly more likely to:

- Engage customers and internal partners
- Get more done in less time
- Support a safe [and reliable] workplace
- Innovate and share ideas
- Have fun while at work[43]

Thankfully, no matter how we in HR connect with our employees, our processes can always be better and have a friendlier approach. We are all fragile, intricate beings. With this multipronged construct, how can a company not be better?

---

[43] Alok Patel and Stephanie Plowman, "The Increasing Importance of a Best Friend at Work," *Gallup*, August 17, 2022, https://www.gallup.com/workplace/397058/increasing-importance-best-friend-work.aspx.

In one company I worked for, I had numerous meetings with a person who had nothing good to say about their leader. The employee disliked their leader's teachings, their leader's standards, and their leader's vision. If it's that bad, why stay? Perhaps it was a belief in the company mission, but that only goes so far. My assessment was that something had happened between them at some point. The employee couldn't get rid of their baggage, and everything the leader did afterwards was seen in a bad light. For that employee to open up, there needed to be psychological safety. Unfortunately, when you have a toxic relationship, it is human nature to recruit others to commiserate with, which is what ultimately happened.

Psychological Safety Sells Everything

People are making decisions and choices based on personal beliefs and values, now more than ever. It is up to leaders to establish the foundation for psychological safety. Employees are not going to make these choices unless the leader does it first, but they will mirror behavior. If the leader leans into uncomfortable vulnerability—being more empathetic, thinking of employees as humans, and making sure people are seen and heard—their employees are going to feel more comfortable doing the same. The leadership lays the groundwork.

I was talking to someone about my OCD, and how I didn't allow myself to worry about how my boss or the wider organization would react. It isn't that I don't care about psychological safety for myself. But because it was so important, I had repressed my feelings. I realized that as an executive I needed to lead by example.

Perhaps I was uncomfortable initially. Protection is a natural human reaction. It's never been in any job description I've seen yet, but I believe that leaders should display vulnerability and transparency. And that vulnerable transparency should include personal examples, at least from time to time. Revealing your humanity elevates the collective humanness, particularly during a crisis (such as a pandemic) when people must be reminded that they are in a secure place. Creating that sense of security can be a deposit of motivation when they need it most. Sometimes you have to be a trailblazer. People have to speak up. It demonstrates a conviction that what you want to speak up about is so important, that you're willing to take the risk.

I will wager a guess that everyone had a little imposter syndrome pre-pandemic. You had your personal life, and you had your work life, and they existed in separate places, literally. Then a lot of people were Zoomed into a corner and forced to do things differently—work and live in the same place. There was no divide, only exposure. Colleagues saw the art on walls and the mess in the bedroom office. Spouses, babies, and pets became famous. Ironically, life is better now for a lot of people because of the pandemic, particularly regarding their work and personal life integration.

Leading as a human being first will create a protective environment for more engagement, and there will be more check-ins outside of specific milestones and success factors. This is what I told Liz Brody, who interviewed me for a piece in *Entrepreneur* magazine four months into a quarantine that shuttered office spaces in every continent for the first time during my career.

Track goals, not hours. The old workweek may slip into obscurity for some industries. Employees might, say, take off Wednesday for a kid's play and catch up on Sunday. This kind of goal-based work—as opposed to hour-based work—is something employees have wanted for ages. Companies have resisted it, stuck in their outdated office mentality, but Wolfe believes that the companies who embrace it will drive engagement and boost loyalty.

To keep a team on task in this new time-shifted world, managers should break up projects into short- and long-term deliverables, with clear systems to communicate who's hitting them. 'Giving people the ability to manage their work lives is a really powerful thing,' he says.[44]

Do you know why this means of protection is so powerful? The practice extends to families, of which your employees are very protective. Every single day, they evaluate their ability to spend time with their loved ones, how their work commitments coincide, and how to allow for *family first*.

---

[44] Liz Brody, "3 Ways to Manage a Team and Talent from Afar," *Entrepreneur*, July 7, 2020, https://www.entrepreneur.com/growing-a-business/3-ways-to-manage-a-team-and-talent-from-afar/352204.

AN EMPATHETIC, EXPRESSIVE LEADER'S PLAYBOOK
Protect and Serve
Maureen Lippe

I talked to Maureen Lippe, founder of Lippe Taylor, an award-winning PR and digital media agency. Lippe Taylor is based in New York City, the competitive epicenter of modern communications. Even after establishing the firm as a thirty-year force of industry, Maureen found that the challenges of the past few years brought new opportunities to "protect and serve with purpose and mindfulness," as she said when we talked about empathetic, expressive leadership.

"When I thought about my younger colleagues living in tiny apartments, unable to see family members during COVID-19, I would continuously write to them, worried day and night about their mental and emotional well-being," she said. "We set up therapists immediately for all staff to use. Their mental wellness was more important than their professional ability at this time. If they are falling apart at home and filled with fear and anxiety, we have to take care of them and offer them immediate HELP. We have to be there for them in every way possible. We are a 'people first company.' And still, it pains me to say... we had many colleagues who experienced a lot of suffering, losing loved ones and being unable to figure things out during this pandemic.

"We thought it most important to stay very close and communicate daily with our colleagues. Our message was 'take care of yourself and take care of each other.' We are a company of healing, empathy, mindfulness, resilience, and intentional listening. This is how our company was able to stay together and heal—emphasis on *together*. During Spring 2021, when we thought we were getting out of this pandemic and could come to work more often, we were set back by the continuation of this dreadful pandemic and the effects long term COVID-19 would have on our entire staff as well as the leadership team. Empathetic leadership, strategy, innovation, self-awareness, as well as accountability, were all important considerations at this lifecycle of Lippe Taylor.

"It was understood that mental fitness and emotional wellness correlated to producing at a high level. To give our people an emotional break, three days a week, we would have black-out hours where everyone was expected to get off their computers; no calls and no meetings were allowed on Friday. We initiated 'PTO at your discretion.' We also surveyed the workforce quarterly to determine their level of mental safety, happiness, and what the company could do better to make them feel whole again. Our CEO had a high EQ, communicated frequently with the staff, was very transparent about our numbers, and carefully worked on the concept of 'belonging' as an everyday priority.

"To not give in to the Great Resignation, we had to first protect our staff, and make sure they know our mission is one of 'purpose and service' to them. 'Empathy and caring,' plus creating a workplace where employees can perform exceptionally well, feeling connection and an authentic sense of humanity is at the heart of what Lippe Taylor stands for. Add clear accountability throughout the process. We have found that this enhances morale and companies reap the rewards of increased workplace productivity and retention, building strong personal connections amongst staff and management. Courage, confidence, kindness, being very aware of your emotional intelligence, and building strong and respectful relationships can be transformational, allowing you to thrive in the workplace as well as your personal life. It's time to embrace EQ 2.0."

Maureen's handle on protecting staff is astounding. I'm sure it wasn't easy or convenient to always communicate so freely and vividly about the company's performance and future. I also appreciate how the focus of her company became trustworthy, flexible schedules, and empowerment, while still producing results.

Would more than forty million people still have resigned, amid a pandemic and a lot of unknowns, if they felt safer at work? If they felt protected by their leaders? We can't know the answer, or change the past. All we can do is be better moving forward.

"My humanity is bound up in yours,
for we can only be human together."

—DESMOND TUTU,
Nobel Peace Prize Recipient

CONCLUSION

Being Better ‖
Better Being

I hope you are allowing yourself to have human reactions to expanding your knowledge on the eight practices of empathetic, expressive leadership. You were curious enough to finish, and you've grown a new or refreshed understanding of what it's like to be a human being. We all have these titles that we use to describe ourselves—Chief HR Officer, Mom, Director of Marketing, Sister, Account Supervisor—but we are all human beings first.

While I've mainly talked to leaders and HR professionals in this book, I want this message to reach all human beings. You do you; be human. We are intricate, fragile beings with the intelligence, power, and passion to make this world a better place. We only need to remember that we are scientifically more alike than we are different.

Let's envision a world where we all see ourselves and each other as human beings first. Our bodies may not look the same, but they are all made of the same stuff, and we have similar feelings and thoughts. It is our experiences, opinions, and views of the world that make us different. We will not always agree, but we can all try to put our humanity first.

Imagine a place where we could stop and converse with someone. We could get to know them before we judge them because of what they look like, how they sound, or what political beliefs they have. We could ask questions to better understand our differences, becoming better acquainted with them and with ourselves. That would be amazing! It will take great effort, consistency, dedication, and potentially feeling uncomfortable. However, do not let any of those reasons stop you from doing it.

I would like to issue a challenge to all of you: the next time you feel that you are judging someone for any reason, stop and think about why you are doing it. If you want to make the world a better place, ask them questions to understand them a bit more. It's quite possible you'll make a connection with them. We can become better leaders, better employees, better spouses, better friends, and better human beings by simply leaving space for people to tell us their stories.

Being human is not difficult. Treating someone well is not hard. These fundamentals have gotten pushed to the back of high-end leadership summits. What's the wow factor? So much time and money have been spent on the breadth of systems and processes. But processes and systems do not focus on the human aspect; they test our brain capacity and finesse our routines with time management tools. Certainly, some of that is helpful, but it doesn't get to the heart of the matter. Going back to our cake analogy, the human aspects are the sprinkles and icing. Wait, even better—they're like a mirror glaze (super fancy, look them up)! When you're treating everyone as a human being, everything builds upon that strong foundation of simple yellow cake.

We all want a boss who we respect and who is respectful to us in turn, who we can confide in, be vulnerable with, and who cares about our career journey enough to advocate for us— or at least most do. Let's continue to talk about that, to help others shine, to shine ourselves by reflecting and sharing our stories, and owning who we are. Sometimes it's not pretty, like my OCD life chapter. Others may have their own mental health factors, trouble at home, or the death of a loved one. But those things are "real," and "real" is what matters in the challenging, gratifying work of being a leader.

On your worst days, please remember that you are a human being first. This reminder alone can distinguish engagement from hot aggression and save you from uttering words you cannot take back. It may stop you from losing sleep or regretting your leadership position. How can you become a better leader? You must start with yourself. You are a human being too: show yourself as one.

Think about what simple change you can make today or tomorrow with your team. Perhaps you tell them how you are doing and ask them how they are. Maybe you put out that dish of candy on your desk to elicit more casual conversations. You could schedule a thirty-minute Ask Me Anything social meeting with each employee that you don't know. Even if you only make one simple change, imagine the impact you will have.

I asked my husband, Drew, if he believed that my extensive travel for work ever took anything away from our time together. I was going to Dublin, London, and Sydney, multiple times a year. Drew also traveled extensively as a travel director, executing plans for corporate meetings and events.

He gave me the best answer possible. "No, because you have the same passion, commitment, and drive at home that you do at work. You have the same level of attention, and you give us your all." Giving my all sometimes means working on my list of seemingly endless projects to do around the house, like installing a flagpole, growing hundreds of peonies, or replacing the recessed lights in the basement with those ones that will "last for decades."

I try to give *myself* my all, too. Sometimes it is as basic as taking an afternoon break to go paddleboarding, making a world-class mojito, or spending time observing the birds while tending to the many feeders in the yard, which feels like a meditative process. Drew, Pam, the dogs, the birds, my friends, my audiences—even you, my readers—they all fuel my quest for making things *better.*

How do you perceive "being better" as an individual? Who needs to be seen? What did you hear when you were listening? How can you show you care? How can you help? How can you protect your life, your people, and your mission? How can you put human beings first? You are already becoming a better human being, just by taking the time to think about it.

Bibliography

Biro, Meghan M. 2022. "Great Employee Return—Or Big Employer
   Mistake?" Forbes. https://www.forbes.com/sites/meghanbiro/
   2022/04/04/great-employee-return---or-big-employer-mistake/.
Bloom, Linda. 2018. "Beware of the Perils of Confirmation Bias."
   Psychology Today. https://www.psychologytoday.com/us/
   blog/stronger-the-broken-places/201807/beware-the-perils-
   confirmation-bias.
Bordeaux, Colleen, and Stephanie Lewis. 2021. "Designing the
   Workforce Experience." Deloitte. https://www2.deloitte.com/us/
   en/blog/human-capital-blog/2021/human-centered-workforce-
   experience.html.
Bordeaux, Colleen, Betsy Grace, and Naina Sabherwal. 2021. "Why
   does belonging matter in the workplace?" Deloitte. https://
   www2.deloitte.com/us/en/blog/human-capital-blog/2021/what-
   is-belonging-in-the-workplace.html.
Brady, Susan M., Janet Foutty, and Lynn P. Wooten. 2022. *Arrive and
   Thrive: 7 Impactful Practices for Women Navigating Leadership*. N.p.:
   McGraw-Hill Education.
Brouk, Tricia. 2021. *The Influential Voice: Saying What You Mean for
   Lasting Legacy*. N.p.: Post Hill Press.
Carnegie, Megan. 2022. "Is workplace stigma around mental health
   struggles changing?" BBC. https://www.bbc.com/worklife/
   article/20220819-is-workplace-stigma-around-mental-health-
   struggles-changing.

Chatzky, Jean. 2018. "5 secrets of success for workers over 50." TODAY. https://www.today.com/money/5-secrets-success-workers-over-50-t141965.

Clark, Timothy R. 2021. "What Psychological Safety Is Not." Forbes. https://www.forbes.com/sites/timothyclark/2021/06/21/what-psychological-safety-is-not/.

Cowen, Alan S., and Keltner Dacher. 2017. "Self-report captures 27 distinct categories of emotion bridged by continuous gradients." PNAS. https://doi.org/10.1073/pnas.1702247114.

Edelman. n.d. "Why we study Trust." Edelman. https://www.edelman.com/trust.

Edmondson, Amy. 1999. "Psychological safety and learning behavior in teams." *Administrative Science Quarterly* 44, no. 2 (June): 250–282. https://web.mit.edu/curhan/www/docs/Articles/15341_Readings/Group_Performance/Edmondson%20Psychological%20safety.pdf.

"Empathy Definition: What Is Empathy." n.d. *Greater Good Magazine.* https://greatergood.berkeley.edu/topic/empathy/definition.

Fisher, Roger, William Ury, Bruce Patton. 1991. *Getting to yes.* Edited by William Ury and Bruce Patton. N.p.: Penguin Books.

Goldberg, Emma. 2022. "Where Did People from the Great Resignation Go? Back to Work." The New York Times. https://www.nytimes.com/2022/05/13/business/great-resignation-jobs.html.

Goleman, Daniel. 2005. *Emotional Intelligence.* N.p.: Bantam Books.

Gulati, Ranjay. 2022. "It's not a Great Resignation–it's a Great Rethink." Fortune. https://fortune.com/2022/03/08/great-resignation-careers-rethink-labor-shortage-pandemic-work-ranjay-gulati/.

Harari, Yuval N. 2015. *Sapiens: A Brief History of Humankind.* Translated by Haim Watzman, Yuval N. Harari, and John Purcell. N.p.: HarperCollins.

Jaffe, Dennis. 2018. "The Essential Importance of Trust: How to Build It or Restore It." Forbes. https://www.forbes.com/sites/dennisjaffe/2018/12/05/the-essential-importance-of-trust-how-to-build-it-or-restore-it/.

Knowledge at Wharton Staff. 2021. "All the Feels: How Companies Can Benefit from Employees' Emotions." Knowledge at Wharton. https://knowledge.wharton.upenn.edu/article/how-companies-can-benefit-from-employees-emotions/.

Krulwich, Robert. 2011. "Leonardo's To-Do List: Krulwich Wonders..." NPR. https://www.npr.org/sections/krulwich/2011/11/18/142467882/leonardos-to-do-list.

Krznaric, Roman. 2014. "Empathy Heroes: 5 People Who Changed the World by Taking Compassion to the Extreme." YES! Magazine. https://www.yesmagazine.org/health-happiness/2014/11/07/empathy-heroes-st-francis-john-howard-griffin-patricia-moore.

Madison, Caleb. 2021. "That Feeling When You 'Feel Seen.'" The Atlantic. https://www.theatlantic.com/newsletters/archive/2021/12/that-feeling-when-you-feel-seen/621050/.

McLeod, Saul. 2022. "Maslow's Hierarchy of Needs." Simply Psychology. https://www.simplypsychology.org/maslow.html.

Mehta, Nick. 2020. "The World Needs Human-first CEOs, Not Wartime CEOs." Gainsight. Accessed September 18, 2022. https://www.gainsight.com/blog/the-world-needs-human-first-ceos-not-war-time-ceos/.

Mental Health America. n.d. "Quick Facts and Statistics About Mental Health." Mental Health America. Accessed September 18, 2022. https://www.mhanational.org/mentalhealthfacts.

Miller-Merrell, Jessica. 2022. "HR Organizational Chart and Department Structures." Workology. https://workology.com/your-guide-to-the-hr-organizational-chart-and-department-structuresstructure-functions/.

Mind Share Partners. 2021. "2021 Mental Health at Work Report—The Stakes Have Been Raised." Mind Share Partners. https://www.mindsharepartners.org/mentalhealthatworkreport-2021.

Patel, Alok, and Stephanie Plowman. 2022. "The Increasing Importance of a Best Friend at Work." Gallup. https://www.gallup.com/workplace/397058/increasing-importance-best-friend-work.aspx.

Psych Safety UK. n.d. "What is Psychological Safety?" Psychological Safety. Accessed September 18, 2022. https://psychsafety.co.uk/about-psychological-safety/.

Riegel, Deborah G. 2020. "26 Easy Ways to Make Your Online Meetings, Workshops, and Programs a Success for Your Small Business." Inc. Magazine. https://www.inc.com/deborah-grayson-riegel/26-easy-ways-to-make-your-online-meetings-workshops-program-a-success-for-your-small-business.html.

Riegel, Deborah G. 2020. "How to Take Initiative in Uncertain Times." Inc. Magazine. https://www.inc.com/deborah-grayson-riegel/how-to-take-initiative-in-uncertain-times.html.

Riegel, Deborah G. 2020. "How to Be a Great Listener in Remote Meetings." Inc. Magazine. https://www.inc.com/deborah-grayson-riegel/how-to-be-a-great-listener-in-remote-meetings.html.

Roberts, Barry. 2016. "Understanding the Chemicals of Leadership and the Impact They Can Have." Wisconsin School of Business. https://business.wisc.edu/news/understanding-the-chemicals-of-leadership-and-the-impact-they-can-have/.

Romanelli, Frank. 2006. "Emotional Intelligence as a Predictor of Academic and/or Professional Success." NCBI. https://www.ncbi.nlm.nih.gov/pmc/articles/PMC1636947/.

"Samantha Lux." n.d. First Event 2023. Accessed September 18, 2022. https://firstevent.org/samantha-lux/.

Schein, Edgar H. 2010. *Organizational Culture and Leadership*. N.p.: Wiley.

SingleCare Team. 2022. "OCD statistics 2022: Facts about obsessive-compulsive disorder." SingleCare. https://www.singlecare.com/blog/news/ocd-statistics/.

Snow, Shane. 2020. "How Psychological Safety Actually Works." Forbes. https://www.forbes.com/sites/shanesnow/2020/05/04/how-psychological-safety-actually-works/.

Snow, Shane. n.d. "Intellectual Humility: The Ultimate Guide to This Timeless Virtue." Shane Snow. Accessed September 22, 2022. https://www.shanesnow.com/articles/intellectual-humility.

Splitter, Jenny, and Justin Laube. 2022. "Can Stress Make You Sick?" Everyday Health. https://www.everydayhealth.com/emotional-health/stress/illnesses-caused-stress/.

Sull, Donald, Charles Sull, and Ben Zweig. 2022. "Toxic Culture Is Driving the Great Resignation." MIT Sloan Management Review. https://sloanreview.mit.edu/article/toxic-culture-is-driving-the-great-resignation/.

Suttie, Jill, and Juliana Breines. 2017. "Why Curious People Have Better Relationships." Greater Good Science Center. https://greatergood.berkeley.edu/article/item/why_curious_people_have_better_relationships.

"What Is Empathy Museum?" n.d. Empathy Museum, Accessed November 27, 2022. https://www.empathymuseum.com/.

"Work With Workology." n.d. Workology. Accessed September 18, 2022. https://workology.com/about/work-with-workology/.

Young Entrepreneur Council. 2016. "11 Unusual Strategies to Boost Engagement in Team Meetings." Inc. Magazine. https://www.inc.com/young-entrepreneur-council/11-unusual-strategies-to-boost-engagement-in-team-meetings.html.

Yu, Alisa, Julian Zlatev, and Justin Berg. 2021. "What's the Best Way to Build Trust at Work?" Harvard Business Review. https://hbr.org/2021/06/whats-the-best-way-to-build-trust-at-work.

About the Author

Paul E. Wolfe is a seasoned CHRO with over 20 years of experience. He is a Board Member at PayScale, as well as a sought-after speaker and advisor. Before his current endeavors, he served as Senior Vice President of Human Resources for Indeed, with a focus on growing, developing, and engaging Indeed's talent while nurturing the company culture. Paul oversaw a multi-disciplined HR group that included HR Business Partners; Talent Attraction; Employee Development; Total Rewards; Diversity, Inclusion, and Belonging; HR Analytics; HR Operations; Employee Experience; and Real Estate. Paul set the talent strategy at Indeed to ensure all current and future business needs were met. He helped them grow from one thousand to over eleven thousand employees in seven years. Paul was also at the forefront of leading the company and its global employee population through the pandemic.

Before Indeed, Paul served as a Vice President, Senior Vice President, and Chief HR Officer of several well-known companies, including Match.com, Orbitz, Condé Nast, and Ticketmaster. Paul holds a bachelor's degree from Nova Southeastern University in Florida. He lives with his husband and their dogs in New York. *Human Beings First* is Paul's debut as an author. Visit *paulwolfe.com*.

Work With Paul

Paul leads workshops and speaks to organizations, companies and teams on a variety of topics in HR and leadership. He especially enjoys supporting leaders to embrace their own humanity, and to reap the rewards of leading with greater empathy. He also makes appearances as an HR expert on major media outlets. Learn more about his keynotes, talks and workshops at **paulwolfe.com**

Ingram Content Group UK Ltd.
Milton Keynes UK
UKHW050648280323
419283UK00011B/108